COPENHAGEN

TOP EXPERIENCES · LOCAL LIFE

CRISTIAN BONETTO

Contents

Plan Your Trip 4

Amalienborg Slot (p82)
FABIAN JUNGE/SHUTTERSTOCK ©

COVID-19

We have re-checked every business in this book before publication to ensure that it is still open after the COVID-19 outbreak. However, the economic and social impacts of COVID-19 will continue to be felt long after the outbreak has been contained, and many businesses, services and events referenced in this guide may experience ongoing restrictions. Some businesses may be temporarily closed, have changed their opening hours and services, or require bookings; some unfortunately could have closed permanently. We suggest you check with venues before visiting for the latest information.

Welcome to Copenhagen

Compact Copenhagen is the epitome of Scandi cool. Modernist lamps light New Nordic tables, bridges buzz with cycling commuters and sporty locals dive into pristine waterways. Despite the cobbled streets, whimsical spires and palaces, this is a city at the very cutting edge, bursting with boundary-pushing food, design and fashion. Go on, take a bite of the (sustainable) good life.

Copenhagen's Top Experiences

Enjoy amusement rides at Tivoli Gardens (p40)

MASSIMO PIZZOTTI/SHUTTERSTOCK ©

Learn some Danish history at Nationalmuseet (p44)

See the ruins of Christiansborg Slot (p52)

OLGAGOROVENKO/SHUTTERSTOCK ©

Admire Danish design at the Designmuseum (p78)

Wander free-spirited Christiania (p90)

NOWACZYK/SHUTTERSTOCK ©

JORDANJOY/SHUTTERSTOCK ©

Visit Christian IV's Renaissance castle (p102)

Relax in Louisiana's seaside sculpture garden (p140)

Explore Denmark's top-tier art museum (p106)

Dining Out

Beneath Copenhagen's galaxy of Michelin stars is an ever-expanding number of hotspots serving contemporary Danish fare at affordable prices. The international food scene has also lifted its game, with a new generation of places offering up authentic dishes. Keeping them company are veritable city institutions serving classic Danish fare.

Old-school Flavours

Reindeer moss and hay-smoked quail eggs may be the norm on New Nordic menus, but traditional Danish tables are a heartier affair. Pork (*flæskor svinekød*) shines in comfort-food favourite *frikadeller*, fried minced-pork meatballs commonly served with boiled potatoes and red cabbage. Equally iconic is the majestic *stjerneskud*. Literally 'shooting star', it's a belt-busting combination of both steamed and fried fish fillets, topped with smoked salmon, shrimp and caviar, and served on buttered bread.

The Sweet Stuff

Ironically, what is known as a 'Danish pastry' abroad is known to the Danes as a *wienerbrød* (Viennese bread). As legend has it, the naming of the pastry can be traced to a Danish baker who moved to Austria in the 18th century, where he perfected the treats of flaky, butter-laden pastry. Not that Denmark's pastry selection ends there. Other famous treats include *kanelsnegle* (cinnamon snail), a scroll sometimes laced with thick, gooey chocolate.

Traditional Danish

Schønnemann An epic repertoire of smørrebrød (pictured) good enough for Michelin-starred chefs. (p68)

Kanal Caféen Salt-of-the-earth staff, epic Danish platters and a canalside location. (p48)

Modern Danish

Kadeau Breathtaking degustations bursting with creativity. (p96)

Høst Sophisticated New Nordic at approachable prices. (p111)

MAKASANA PHOTO/SHUTTERSTOCK ©

Restaurant Mes Subtle foreign twists and whimsical presentation. (p48)

Pluto Seasonal, honest grub in a buzzing, friendly space. (p112)

Seafood

Oysters & Grill Spectacular oysters, shellfish and more at a convivial, casual favourite. (p119)

Kødbyens Fiskebar Creative, high-end sharing plates in a buzzy industrial setting. (p133)

Asian Flavours

District Tonkin Authentic *bánh mì* (Vietnamese baguettes) and northern Vietnamese bites. (p84)

The Market Intriguing pan-Asian flavours in a slinky space. (p68)

Italian Flavours

Bæst Home-made artisan cheeses, charcuterie and wood-fired pizzas from an Italo-Danish powerhouse. (p119)

Fischer Simple, beautiful antipasti and pasta dishes in a low-key neighbourhood bistro. (p125)

Cheap Eats

Hija de Sanchez Real-deal, high-quality tacos from a Noma alumnus. (p133)

Tommi's Burger Joint Lusty burgers in the Meatpacking District. (p135)

Morgenstedet Organic vegetarian food in a bucolic Christiania setting. (p97)

Top Tips

∘ Reserve a table at popular restaurants, especially later in the week. Many of them offer easy online reservations.

∘ If you like to eat late, you'll have trouble finding a place to accommodate you after about 10pm.

Treasure Hunt

What Copenhagen's shopping lacks in size it more than makes up for with quality and individuality. The city is Scandinavia's capital of cool, with no shortage of locally designed and crafted must-haves to rekindle your spending fire. Good buys include unique streetwear and higher-end fashion, ceramics, glassware, jewellery and textiles.

Where to Shop

Strøget offers mostly generic fashion chains, with the more upmarket options at its eastern end (Østergade). Amagertorv is home to flagship stores for Royal Copenhagen, George Jensen and design behemoth Illums Bolighus. More high-street chains line Købmagergade, with the hippest Nordic fashion stores concentrated in the streets east of Købmagergade and north of Østergade (including Gammel Mønt, Grønnegade and Mønter-

gade). A handful of vintage stores dot the Latin Quarter, with some quirky, higher-end fashion stops on Krystalgade.

North of Nyhavn, salubrious Bredgade offers exclusive art and antiques. For more affordable bric-a-brac, vintage jewellery and kitschy objects, scour Ravnsborggade in Nørrebro or explore Nørrebro Loppemarked, the neighbourhood's seasonal Saturday flea market. Nørrebro is also home to Elmegade and Jægersborggade, two streets pimped

with independent shops. Vesterbro is another good bet for independent fashion and homewares, with most of the offerings on and around Istedgade and Værndamsvej.

Best Women's Clothes

Stine Goya Playful, individualistic outfits from Denmark's hottest independent designer. (p113)

Baum und Pferdgarten Bold, colourful, higher-end collections from a Danish duo. (p74)

Storm Harder-to-find labels, accessories and gifts in a unisex concept store. (p74)

RUFENACH/ULLSTEIN BILD VIA GETTY IMAGES ©

Best for Men's Clothes

NN07 High-quality, pared-back clothes and accessories fusing Nordic and Japanese aesthetics. (p74)

Wood Wood Cult-status concept store stocking in-house streetwear, plus guest labels, footwear, eyewear and fragrances. (p75)

Samsøe & Samsøe Super-cool, comfy casualwear from Samsøe as well as guest labels. (p129)

Best for Interior Design

Hay House Contemporary furniture, furnishings and gifts from new-school Scandi talent. (p73)

Illums Bolighus Four floors of design for every room in your house. (p73; pictured)

Gourmet Treats

Torvehallerne KBH A celebrated food market heaving with goods for the pantry and cellar. (p108)

Juuls Vin og Spiritus Stock the cellar with Nordic akvavits, gins and more. (p129)

Local Gifts & Souvenirs

Posterland Awesome selection of posters, including retro ads for Danish beer, transport, cities and more. (p74)

Designmuseum Danmark Cool, easy-to-carry gifts, from local jewellery and Nordic cookbooks to statement-making socks. (p78)

Top Tip

○ Citizens from countries outside the EU can claim a VAT refund on goods as they leave the EU (as long as they spend a minimum of 300kr per shop and the shop participates in one of the refund schemes). Get the shop to fill in a refund form, then present it, together with your passport, receipts and purchases, at the airport upon departure.

Museums & Galleries

Copenhagen is packed with engaging museums and galleries, from the epic to the eclectic. Together they house a seemingly endless array of cultural treasures, from ancient tomb wares and sacrificial bodies to dazzling swords and jewels, iconic modernist design and envelope-pushing contemporary installations from Denmark and beyond.

Plan Your Visit

Many museums and galleries close at least one day a week, usually on Monday. Some stay open late one or more nights a week, often on Wednesday or Thursday. While Nationalmuseet, Statens Museum for Kunst and Davids Samling are always free, some museums – among them Ny Carlsberg Glyptotek and Thorvaldsens Museum – offer free admission once a week, often on Wednesday or Sunday.

Park Museums

Statens Museum for Kunst, Rosenborg Slot, Davids Samling, Hirschsprung, Statens Naturhistoriske Museum (including Geologisk Museum) and Arbejdermuseet together form the Parkmuseerne (www. parkmuseerne.dk) district. A combination ticket (Dkr245) covers all venues and includes a modest 10% discount at the museum stores.

Best for History

Nationalmuseet The country's entire biography under one roof. (p44)

Rosenborg Slot Royal bling in Christian IV's Renaissance summer pad. (p102)

Ruinerne under Christiansborg The ruins of Copenhagen's earliest fortress and castle. (p53)

Designmuseum Danmark Explore the roots of Danish design. (p78)

De Kongelige Stalde An equine affair of carriages, uniforms and riding equipment at the Royal Stables. (p60)

Tøjhusmuseet Analyse historical battles at the Royal Danish Arsenal Museum. (p61)

Best Art Museums

Statens Museum for Kunst Denmark's preeminent art

YULIYA IVANENKO/SHUTTERSTOCK ©

collection spans medieval to modern. (p106)

Louisiana World-class masterpieces with an aside of modernist architecture. (p140)

Ny Carlsberg Glyptotek Egyptian and Mediterranean antiquities plus Impressionist art. (p47; pictured)

Thorvaldsens Museum Denmark's first museum building and a shrine to the nation's greatest sculptor. (p59)

Best Lesser-known Treasures

Davids Samling A neoclassical apartment graced with Eastern and Western treasures. (p111)

Hirschsprung An elegant repository of 19th- and 20th-century Danish art. (p111)

Dansk Jødisk Museum Jewry heritage in a space designed by architect Daniel Libeskind. (p60)

Best Contemporary Art Galleries

Kunsthal Charlottenborg One of Europe's largest venues for modern talent from around the globe. (p83)

Kunstforeningen GL Strand A canalside showcase of forward-thinking local and foreign works. (p66)

V1 Gallery Edgy exhibitions in Vesterbro's vibrant Meatpacking District. (p132)

Top Tip

○ If you plan on blitzing the museums, consider purchasing the **Copenhagen Card** (www.copenhagencard.com; adult/child 10-15yr 24hr 419/209kr, 48hr 619/309kr, 72hr 759/379kr, 96hr 889/449kr, 120hr 999/499kr), which offers free entry to over 80 museums and attractions, as well as free public transport. Sights covered include Rosenborg Slot, Nationalmuseet and Ny Carlsberg Glyptotek.

Under the Radar

While most Copenhagen hit lists include world-famous Nyhavn, Tivoli Gardens and the (underwhelming) Little Mermaid statue, the curious veer off the main tourist trails. Their reward is a more genuine slice of Copenhagen life, one filled with unique neighbourhoods, artisan studios and tranquil gardens made for perfect picnics.

Local Neighbourhoods

Exploring less touristy neighbourhoods allows you to tap into the city the locals know, to better understand Copenhagen, its people and nuances, and to support smaller neighbourhood businesses.

Multicultural **Nørrebro** is home to some 60 different nationalities, not to mention a large community of artists and students. Streets like Jægersborggade, Blågårdsgade and Elmegade buzz with in-dependent boutiques, galleries, restaurants, cafes and bars. At the northern end of Nør-rebrogade (Nørrebro's main thoroughfare) is Superkilen, an imaginative, one-of-a-kind park celebrating the neighbourhood's diversity. In chi-chi **Østerbro**, colourful Brumleby and Olufsvej are gorgeous heritage areas, while leafy, cafe-flanked Bopa Plads (Bopa Square) is a popular hangout for Østerbro locals.

Beyond **Vester-bro**'s Kødbyen (Meat-packing District),

make time to explore the neighbour-hood's village-like Værnedamsvej, as well as Vesterbro's gi-ant street-art murals. West of Vesterbro lies salubrious **Frederiks-berg**, home to the romantic Frederiksberg Have district, extraordinary subterranean art gallery Cisternerne and cult-status flea market Frederiksberg Loppetorv.

Best Off-Track Sights

Davids Samling Superb Islamic and European art, hidden away in a collector's former townhouse. (p111)

OLIVER FOERSTNER/SHUTTERSTOCK ©

Assistens Kirkegård Burial place of Hans Christian Andersen, and a much-loved picnic spot. (p119; pictured)

Cisternerne Moody, subterranean reservoir turned contemporary art space in Frederiksberg. (p139)

Best Neighbourhood Shopping

Vanishing Point Thoughtfully curated local crafts and gifts, from quirky ceramics to hand-knitted sweaters. (p123)

Gågrøn! Useful, sustainable Danish items like organic soaps, candles and biodynamic woollen socks. (p123)

Frederiksberg Loppetorv Frederiksberg's Saturday flea market draws curious locals and serious collectors alike. (p139)

Best Neighbourhood Hangouts

Brus Cult-status craft beers and superb bites in a big, old Nørrebro factory. (p121)

Pixie The quintessential neighbourhood cafe-bar, on a leafy Østerbro square. (p125)

Bankeråt Kooky Nørreport bar with offbeat interiors and a homely, unpretentious vibe. (p113)

Reffen ⓘ

A short bike ride north of Operæn (or a harbour bus ferry trip to Refshaleøn ferry stop) lies Reffen (reffen.dk), a hip waterfront street-food market peddling sustainable, organic bites.

Bar Open

Copenhagen's vibrant drinking areas include Vesterbro's Kødbyen (Meat-packing District), Istedgade and the northern end of Viktoriagade; Nørrebro's Ravnsborggade, Elmegade, Sankt Hans Torv and Jægersborggade; and the historic Latin Quarter.

A is for Akvavit

Denmark's most popular spirit is the Aalborg-produced akvavit. There are several dozen types, the most common of which is made from potatoes and spiced with caraway seeds. In Denmark akvavit is not sipped but is swallowed straight down as a shot, usually followed by a chaser of øl (beer).

It's Øl Good

Copenhagen's first brewing guild was established in 1525 and its homegrown breweries include commercial giant Carlsberg and craft brewer Mikkeller. The latter is one of several independents producing innovative beers in a wide variety of styles. While the bestselling beers in Denmark are pilsners, a lager with an alcohol content of 4.6%, there are scores of beers to choose from. These range from light beers with an alcohol content of 1.7% to hearty stouts that kick in at 8%. Thirsty? Remember these handy terms: *lyst øl* (light beer), *lagerøl* (dark lager), *fadøl* (draught), *porter* (stout) and *bryghus* (brewery or brew pub).

For Cocktails

Ruby Meticulous, made-from-scratch cocktails at a world-renowned bar. (p70)

Lidkoeb Beautiful libations in a hidden location right off Vesterbrogade. (p135)

1105 A dark, sleek city-centre cocktail den for grown-ups. (p70)

For Wine

Ved Stranden 10 Knowledgeable staff pouring unusual drops. (p69)

RADIOKAFKA/SHUTTERSTOCK ©

Nebbiolo Trendy Italian enoteca with top wine just off Nyhavn. (p86)

Den Vandrette Natural wines and summertime harbourside tables. (p86)

Falernum Plenty of wines by the glass on a Parisian-esque Vesterbro strip. (p129)

For Craft Beer

Brus Twenty-four rotating beers on tap, including standout local brews. (p121)

Mikkeller & Friends Craft brews, plus Belgian-style beers in a back bar. (p121; pictured)

Nørrebro Bryghus Organic craft beers from a maverick urban microbrewery. (p122)

For Coffee

Coffee Collective Copenhagen's most revered specialty micro-roastery. (p122)

Sort Kaffe & Vinyl Record store and coffee shop in ever-hip Vesterbro. (p137)

Democratic Coffee Smooth specialty brews in the erudite Latin Quarter. (p71)

Nyhavn For Less

Skip Nyhavn's touristy canalside bars and buy your beers and wine cheaper at seasonal convenience store Turs Havneproviant on nearby Lille Strandstræde 3. Stocked up, enjoy your drinks by the canal. It's legal.

Show Time

ARCHITECT: HENNING LARSEN;
IMAGE: AGEHRIG/SHUTTERSTOCK ©

Copenhagen's entertainment offerings are wide, varied and sophisticated. On any given night choices will include ballet, opera, theatre, clubbing and live tunes spanning indie and blues to pop. The city has a world-renowned jazz scene, with numerous jazz clubs drawing top talent. Note: many nightspots don't get the party started until 11pm.

Live Music & DJs

Vega Three venues in one, serving up an alphabet of genres. (p137)

Rust A classic spot for indie rock, pop, hip-hop and electronica. (p122)

Culture Box Electronic music spun by A-list local and global DJs. (p113)

Loppen Raw, feverish, alternative acts in a scruffy Christiania warehouse. (p92)

Jazz & Blues

Jazzhus Montmartre A veteran jazz peddler, with decent pre-show dining. (p71)

Mojo Moody nightly tunes spanning blues to soul, plus an affable, welcoming vibe. (p49)

Performing Arts

Det Kongelige Teater Encore-worthy ballet and opera in Copenhagen's most opulent period theatre. (p86)

Skuespilhuset Contemporary home of the Royal Danish Theatre, with classic and modern productions. (p87)

Operaen Sterling opera in a showstopping harbourside landmark. (p99; pictured)

For Cinephiles

Cinemateket Quality independent cinema, including bimonthly Danish film classics. (p73)

Top Tip

o Located at the main Tivoli Gardens entrance, **Tivoli Box Office** (☑33 15 10 01; Vesterbrogade 3; ⏱10am-10.45 Sun-Thu, to 11.45pm Fri & Sat during Tivoli seasons, 10am-6pm Mon-Fri rest of year; ☒2A, 9A, 5C, 12, 14, 26, 66, 250S, ⑤København H) not only sells Tivoli performance tickets, it's also an agent for **BilletNet** (☑70 15 65 65; www.ticketmaster. dk), which sells tickets for concerts, theatre, comedy, sporting events and music festivals.

Hygge

CHETTARIN/SHUTTERSTOCK ©

While it might be a little unusual to call a feeling a city highlight, in the case of Danish hygge, we heartily recommend that you grab a piece of the action. What is hygge? How do you achieve it? And just how does it feel? Light some candles, pour a warming cup of coffee, and read on.

Hygge: 101

While there is really no equivalent in English, *hygge* loosely refers to a sense of friendly, warm companionship of a kind fostered when Danes gather together in groups of two or more. The participants don't even have to be friends, but if the conversation flows – avoiding potentially divisive topics like politics and the best way to pickle a herring – the bonhomie blossoms, and toasts are raised before an open fire (or, at the very least, some tealights), you are probably coming close.

Old-School Hygge

Tivoli Gardens A mood-lifting jumble of carnival rides, twinkling lights and old-fashioned charm. (p40)

La Glace Snuggle up with hot tea and a luscious slice of walnut cake. (p69; pictured)

For Hip Hygge

Kind of Blue A moody, vinyl-playing neighbourhood bar with a bluesy, Mississippi soul. (p122)

Oysters & Grill Convivial, tavern-spirited favourite serving share-friendly seafood and more. (p119)

Lidkoeb Sheepskin, candles and a festive courtyard set a *hyggelig* scene for superlative libations. (p135)

Bastard Café Hipsters and geeks relive their wonder years over board games and drinks. (p70)

Top Tip

∘ Danish *hygge* reaches fever pitch in December, when twinkling lights, flowing *gløgg* (mulled wine) and Tivoli Garden's famous Christmas market crank up the cosiness and camaraderie.

For Free

VATOLSTIKOFF/SHUTTERSTOCK ©

While Copenhagen is hardly a bargain destination, the city does spoil the well-informed with free thrills, including some of its most impressive sights. Some are always free, while others are free on specific days of the week. The city's compact size means it's easy enough to save money on transport, keeping costs lower and your spirits higher.

Best Always-Free Museums

Davids Samling A dazzling booty of Islamic treasures, and European paintings and applied arts. (p111)

Best Sometimes-Free Museums

Ny Carlsberg Glyptotek From Egyptian tombs to French impressionists, an eclectic cultural hoard that's free on Tuesdays. (p47)

Thorvaldsens Museum Wednesdays cost nada at this ode to Denmark's most accomplished sculptor. (p59)

Nikolaj Kunsthal The contemporary art exhibitions inside this former church are free on Wednesdays. (p67)

Best Free Experiences

Assistens Kirkegård Enjoy one-on-one time with some of Denmark's most illustrious historical figures. (p119)

Islands Brygge Havnebadet Work it, flaunt it or just get it wet at Copenhagen's hottest harbour pool complex. (p99)

Christiania Soak up the sights, sounds and scents of Copenhagen's most unconventional neighbourhood. (p90)

Christiansborg Slot Tower The million-dollar view from Copenhagen's tallest tower is complimentary. (p54; pictured)

Botanisk Have Wander through the largest collection of living plants in Denmark. (p111)

Top Tip

○ **Copenhagen Free Walking Tours** (www.copenhagenfreewalkingtours.dk) runs a three-hour Grand Tour of Copenhagen several times weekly, departing from outside Rådhus. A 90-minute Christianshavn tour departs several times weekly from Højbro Plads. Tours are technically free though a tip is expected; see the website for times.

Tours

TRABANTOS/SHUTTERSTOCK ©

Overview Tours

Netto-Bådene (☎32 54 41 02; www.havnerundfart. dk; Holmens Bro; adult/child 40/15kr; ☺tours 2-5 per hour, 10am-7pm Jul & Aug, reduced hours rest of year; ♿; ☐1A, 2A, 9A, 26, 37, 66) The cheapest of Copenhagen's harbour and canal tours, with embarkation points at Holmens Kirke and Nyhavn.

Canal Tours Copenhagen (☎32 96 30 00; www. stromma.dk; Nyhavn; 1hr tour adult/child 85/43kr; ☺9.30am-9pm late Jun–mid-Aug, reduced hours rest of year; ☐1A, 26, 66, 350S, Ⓜ Kongens Nytorv; pictured) Highly popular one-hour harbour and canal tours departing from Nyhavn and Ved Stranden.

Copenhagen City Sightseeing (☎32 96 30 00; www.citysightseeing. dk; tickets adult/child from 158/79kr; ☺departures every 30-60min, 9.30am-4.30pm daily late Apr–mid-

Sep, shorter hours & routes rest of year) A hop-on, hop-off bus with three routes to choose from. The two-day 'Bus & Boat combo' also covers Canal Tours Copenhagen.

Active Tours

Kayak Republic (☎22 88 49 89; www.kayakrepublic. dk; Børskaj 12; 1/2/3hr rental 175/275/375kr, 2hr guided tour 395kr; ☺10am-9pm Jun-Aug, reduced hours rest of year; ☐2A, 9A, 37, 350S) Two-hour tours along the city's canals, as well as less-frequent, three-hour tours focused on Nordic food or architecture. Located just beside Christian IV's Bro.

Bike Copenhagen With Mike (☎26 39 56 88; www. bikecopenhagenwithmike. dk; Sankt Peders Stræde 47; per person 300kr; ☐5C, 6A) Idiosyncratic three-hour cycling tours of Copenhagen, departing from Sankt Peders Stræde 47 in the city centre. Seasonal and private tours

are also available; see the website.

Running Tours Copenhagen (☎50 59 17 29; www.runningtours.dk; 1-2 people 350kr, each additional person 150kr; ☐2A, 12, 14, 26, 33, 250S, Ⓢ København H) Run or jog your way through the city and its history. Tours commence in Rådhuspladsen.

Themed Tours

Nordic Noir Tours (www. nordicnoirtours.com; per person from 200kr; ☺private tours by request, semi-private tours by pre-booking only: Borgen tour 2pm Sat, The Killing/The Bridge tour 4pm Sat; ☐6A, 12, 31, 34, 37, 66, Ⓢ Vesterport) Retrace the steps of your favourite Nordic TV characters from *Borgen*, *The Bridge* and *The Killing* on these 90-minute location walking tours. Tours depart from Vesterport S-train station.

For Kids

Copenhagen seems tailor-made for little ones. And we're not just talking about its world-famous, centrally located amusement park, Tivoli Gardens. We're talking about free entry for kids at most museums, engaging cultural institutions with special family activities, child-friendly parks and beaches, and a transport system that actually considers prams.

EVIKKA/SHUTTERSTOCK ©

For Artistic Inspiration

Louisiana Museum of Modern Art Superlative modern art museum with a huge children's wing and plenty of outdoor running space. (p140)

Statens Museum for Kunst Denmark's National Gallery offers a sketching room, weekend workshops for kids, plus a monthly kids' day. (p106)

Outdoor Thrills

Tivoli Gardens The world's most charming amusement park, with laser shows, fireworks and rides from the tame to the insane. (p40; pictured)

GoBoat Kids can play 'trash pirates' on solar-powered boats, collecting rubbish for a reward. (p97)

Islands Brygge Havnebadet Wade, bomb or swim with a summertime dip at Copenhagen's favourite harbour pool. (p99)

Kongens Have Catch a summertime puppet show in Christian IV's old backyard. (p105)

For Historical Insight

Nationalmuseet Sail a ship or be a knight in the National Museum's interactive Children's Museum. (p44)

Rosenborg Slot Stomp through a gingerbread-style castle, complete with guards, moat and basement crowns. (p102)

Top Tips

o Larger bicycle-rental outfits have kids' trailers and kids' bikes for rent.

o Kids aged 12 to 15 years pay half-price on public transport. An adult with a valid ticket can take two children under the age of 12 for free.

o See www.visitcopenhagen.com for family-friendly activities.

Architecture

Copenhagen's architectural cache is rich and diverse, spanning many centuries and architectural styles. Despite its age, this is a city not short of contemporary edge, its Renaissance, baroque and National Romantic treasures sharing the spotlight with modernist icons and innovative just-built marvels that inspire urban planners across the globe.

ARCHITECTS: SCHMIDT HAMMER LASSEN:
IMAGE: BALIPADMA/SHUTTERSTOCK ©

Historical Overview

Copenhagen's architectural legacy begins with Bishop Absalon's 12th-century fortress, its ruins visible beneath Christiansborg Slot. 'Builder King' Christian IV embarked on an extraordinary building program in the 17th century that includes Børsen, Rundetårn and Rosenborg Slot. Rococo delights include Amalienborg Slot and Marmorkirken, while Rådhus (City Hall) is a standout example of the National Romantic style – inspired by Scandinavian heritage and popular at the turn of last century.

Rosenborg Slot A petite castle built in the Dutch Renaissance style. (p102)

Christiansborg Slot Copenhagen's boldest neo-baroque statement. (p52)

Rundetårn Christian IV's astronomical tower, complete with equestrian staircase. (p66)

Børsen A Dutch Renaissance stock exchange with rooftop dragons. (p59)

Det Kongelige Bibliotek The 'Black Diamond' heralded a new era for Copenhagen's waterfront. (p59; pictured)

Operaen Copenhagen's harbourfront opera house divides opinion. (p99)

Top Tip

Located in Dutch architect Rem Koolhaas' Blox building, the **Dansk Arkitektur Center** (p59) houses a notable book and design store, hosts exhibitions on architecture, and also runs architecture-themed walking tours of the city. See the website for dates and details.

Danish Design

Is there a more design-conscious nation than Denmark, or a more design-obsessed capital than Copenhagen? From its restaurant and hotel interiors to its cycling overpasses, one of Copenhagen's most inspirational qualities is its love and mastery of the applied arts.

EQROY/SHUTTERSTOCK ©

Kaare Klint: Danish Design Pioneer

While modern Danish design bloomed in the 1950s, its roots are firmly planted in the 1920s and the work of pioneering Danish modernist Kaare Klint (1888–1954). The architect spent much of his career studying the human form and modified a number of chair designs for added functionality. Klint's obsession with functionality, accessibility and attention to detail would ultimately drive and define Denmark's mid-20th-century design scene and its broader design legacy.

Designmuseum Danmark Delve into the history and iconic pieces of Denmark's design heritage. (p78)

Klassik Moderne Møbelkunst A retail repository for the country's most celebrated chairs, tables and more. (p87)

Hay House Furniture, homeware and gifts from new-school Nordic talent. (p73)

Illums Bolighus All the biggest names in design on four inspiring levels. (p73)

Høst The urban-rustic interior of this New Nordic nosh spot has swagged international awards. (p111)

Dansk Arkitektur Center Sharply curated exhibitions exploring architecture and urban design. (p59; pictured)

Top Tip

The annual **3 Days of Design** (http://3days ofdesign.dk) festival sees dozens of venues, from furniture and design stores to cafes and Designmuseum Danmark, host special design-themed events open to the public. These include talks, tours and product launches. See the website for details.

Festivals & Events

OLIVER FOERSTNER/SHUTTERSTOCK ©

Bass-thumping block parties and saxy jazz, pot-stirring celebrity chefs, groundbreaking films and documentaries, and a rainbow-coloured Pride parade: Copenhagen's social calendar is a buzz-inducing, toe-tapping affair. Sunshine, sleet or snow, you're bound to find a reason to head out and celebrate the finer things in life.

Best for Culture Vultures

Kulturnatten (Culture Night; www.kulturnatten. dk; ☺Oct) Late-night art and culture, usually in mid-October.

Kulturhavn (www. kulturhavn.dk; ☺Aug) Three days of mostly free harbourside events in August.

Best for Music

Copenhagen Jazz Festival (www.jazz.dk; ☺Jul; pictured) Over three weeks of world-class jazz in July. A winter edition is held in February.

Copenhagen Blues Festival (www.copenhagen bluesfestival.dk; ☺Sep/Oct) Three days of interna-

tional blues in late September or early October.

Strøm (www.stromcph.dk; ☺Aug) A four-day electronic music festival in August.

Distortion (www.cph distortion.dk; ☺May/Jun) Five heady days of club and block parties in late May or early June.

Best for Gluttons

Copenhagen Cooking (www.copenhagencooking. dk; ☺Aug) Scandinavia's largest food festival runs in August.

Copenhagen Beer Week (www.thefoodproject.dk) Showcases Danish brewers over nine days in September.

Best for Film Buffs

CPH:PIX (www.cphpix.dk; ☺Autumn) Copenhagen's feature film festival runs in autumn.

CPH:DOX (www.cphdox. dk; ☺Mar/Apr) An acclaimed, 12-day documentary film festival running in March and April.

Top Tip

The best source of up-to-date information on events is www.visitcopenhagen.com. Also useful is the English-language Copenhagen Post (www.cphpost.dk).

Four Perfect Days

Day One

SOFIA POPOVYCH/SHUTTERSTOCK ©

Pique your appetite at **Torve-hallerne KBH** (p108; pictured), Copenhagen's celebrated food market. Walk over to **Kongens Have** (p105), a former royal backyard turned city park. Snoop around the Hogwarts-worthy rooms of its 17th-century castle, **Rosenborg Slot** (p102), home to the Danish crown jewels.

Continue east to salty **Nyhavn** (p82). Walk north along the harbourfront to royal pad **Amalienborg Slot** (p82), the glorious church **Marmorkirken** (p83) and, further north, fortress **Kastellet** (p83). If you must, the **Little Mermaid** awaits a short walk away from Kastellet. Once done, catch a Harbour Bus south to **Det Kongelige Bibliotek** (p59). Spend the evening at **Tivoli Gardens** (p40).

Day Two

POLUDZIBER/SHUTTERSTOCK ©

Start on a high by climbing **Rundetårn** (p66; pictured), a 17th-century tower. The streets directly to the east are dotted with Nordic fashion boutiques, such as **Wood Wood** (p75) and **Han Kjøbenhavn** (p75), as well as Scandi design stores like **Hay House** (p73). Alternatively, explore the **Latin Quarter** (p66). It's here that you'll find **Vor Frue Kirke** (p66), home to sculptures by the great Bertel Thorvaldsen.

You could easily spend the afternoon exploring Danish history at the **Nationalmuseet** (p44). Alternatively, opt for **Ny Carlsberg Glyptotek** (p47). Continue the night at **Ved Stranden 10** (p69), innovative cocktails at **Ruby** (p70) or some evening sax at **Jazzhus Montmartre** (p71).

Day Three

RADIOKAFKA/SHUTTERSTOCK ©

Spend the morning exploring Christianshavn. Pop into **Christians Kirke** (p96) and **Vor Frelsers Kirke** (p95). Both are within walking distance of **Christiania** (p90).

Cross the Knippels Bridge to reach Slotsholmen. The island's protagonist is **Christiansborg Slot** (p52), whose breathtaking **De Kongelige Repræsentationslokaler** (p53) are worth a visit. Directly below are the **Ruinerne under Christiansborg** (p53). Drop into **Thorvaldsens Museum** (p59).

Kick back in Kødbyen, home to numerous bars – including **Mesteren & Lærlingen** (p136) – wrap things up at craft-beer standouts **Mikkeller Bar** (p136; pictured) and **Fermentoren** (p137), or cocktail hideout **Lidkoeb** (p135).

Day Four

GETPHOTO/SHUTTERSTOCK ©

Delve into masterpieces both old and cutting edge at **Statens Museum for Kunst** (p106). If you need to clear your head, the canvas-worthy **Botanisk Have** (p111) is just across the road.

Spend the afternoon exploring Copenhagen's densest, coolest, most multicultural neighbourhood, Nørrebro. When it's time to pause, people-watch in out-of-the-box urban park **Superkilen** (p117; pictured) or take a nap in dreamy **Assistens Kirkegård** (p119).

Keep the night rolling at Nørrebro's drinking holes, among them craft-beer hotspots **Brus** (p121) and **Mikkeller & Friends** (p121) or the perennially soulful **Kind of Blue** (p122). For live music and late-week clubbing sessions, hit **Rust** (p122).

Need to Know

For detailed information, see Survival Guide (p143)

Currency
Danish krone (kr)

Language
Danish; English widely spoken

Money
ATMs widely available. Credit cards accepted in most hotels, restaurants and shops. Some businesses accept cards, not cash.

Mobile Phones
Mobile coverage is widespread. Non-EU residents should bring a GSM-compatible phone; local SIM cards are available.

Time
Central European Time (GMT/UTC plus one hour)

Tipping
Rare and not expected at hotels. Consider tipping 10% of the bill for exceptional service at restaurants and consider rounding up the fare in taxis.

Daily Budget

Budget: Less than 800kr
Dorm bed: 150–300kr
Double room in budget hotel: 500–700kr
Cheap meal: under 125kr

Midrange: 800–1500kr
Double room in midrange hotel: 700–1500kr
Museum admission: 50–150kr
Three-course menu 300-400kr

Top end: More than 1500kr
Double room in top-end hotel: 1500kr and up
Degustation menu at Kadeau: 1800kr

Advance Planning

Two months before Book your hotel and a table at restaurant Kadeau.

One to two weeks before Secure a table at hotspot restaurants like Restaurant Mes, Bror and Høst.

Few days before Scan www.visitcopenhagen.com and www.aok.dk for upcoming events.

Useful Websites

Visit Copenhagen (www.visitcopenhagen.com) Covers everything from accommodation and sightseeing to dining, shopping and events.

Rejseplanen (www.rejseplanen.dk) Useful journey planner.

Lonely Planet (www.lonelyplanet.com/copenhagen) Destination information, hotel bookings, traveller forum and more.

Arriving in Copenhagen

Most people arrive by air, landing at Copenhagen Airport, Scandinavia's busiest international airport. A smaller number of international visitors arrive in Copenhagen by train to Central Station, by long-distance bus or by ferry.

From Copenhagen Airport

Trains run to the city centre around every 10 to 20 minutes, with fewer services overnight. Metro trains also run to the city centre every four to 20 minutes, 24 hours a day. Taxis to the city centre cost around 250kr to 300kr.

From Central Station

All regional and international trains arrive at and depart from Central Station (København H), located in the heart of the city. Trains run to the airport every 10 to 20 minutes, with less frequent services overnight. Most long-distance buses terminate on Ingerslevsgade, at the southern end of Central Station.

From Søndre Frihavn

Cruise ferries to and from Norway dock at Søndre Frihavn, located 2km north of Kongens Nytorv. Bus 26 connects the port to the city centre and Vesterbro.

Getting Around

⚲ Bike

Most streets have cycle lanes and motorists tend to respect them. Bikes can be carried free on S-trains, but are forbidden at Nørreport station during weekday peak times. Bikes are also banned on the metro during weekday peak times.

🚌 Bus

Extensive coverage. Primary routes have an 'A' after their route number and run 24 hours a day, every three to seven minutes in peak times and every 10 minutes at other times. Night buses (marked with an 'N' after their route number) run between 1am and 5am.

Ⓜ Metro

Two lines, M1 and M2. Services run around the clock: every two to four minutes in peak times, three to six minutes during the day and on weekends, and seven to 20 minutes at night. Line M2 runs to the airport.

🚃 Train

Runs seven lines through Central Station (København H). Services run every four to 20 minutes from approximately 5am to 12.30am. All-night services run hourly on Friday and Saturday (half-hourly on line F).

⚓ Ferry

The city's commuter ferries are known as Harbour Buses. There are 10 stops along the harbourfront.

Copenhagen Neighbourhoods

Nørrebro (p115)
Copenhagen at its graffiti-scrawled best, jam-packed with indie cafes, rocking retro treasures and buried national legends.

Nørreport (p101)
An appetite-piquing, soul-stirring feast of market produce, artistic masterpieces, royal turrets and jewels, and dashing parklands.

Vesterbro (p127)
The pinnacle of Copenhagen cool, where post-industrial bars, eateries and galleries mix with vintage second-hand shops.

Tivoli Gardens

Nyhavn & the Royal Quarter (p77)

Masts and maritime buildings, a rococo royal palace and the world's most famous mermaid – welcome to the city of postcard images.

Strøget & Around (p63)

Nordic fashion flagships, buzzing cafes and bars, and twisting cobbled streets draw the crowds to Copenhagen's historic heart.

Statens Museum for Kunst

Designmuseum Danmark

Rosenborg Slot

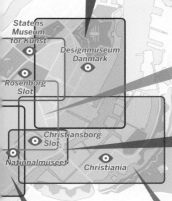

Slotsholmen (p51)

Parliamentary palace, medieval ruins, blue-blooded artefacts and a gobsmacking library: tiny Slotsholmen packs a powerful punch.

Christiansborg Slot

Nationalmuseet

Christiania

Tivoli Area (p39)

Copenhagen's bustling 'welcome mat', home to the cultural blockbuster Nationalmuseet and ageless charmer Tivoli Gardens.

Christianshavn (p89)

Scandinavia's answer to Amsterdam, pimped with cosy canals, boats and cafes, and the pot-scented streets of alt-living commune Christiania.

Explore
Copenhagen

Worth a Trip 👀

Copenhagen's Walking Tours 🥾

Nyhavn (p77) ELROCE/SHUTTERSTOCK ©

Explore ⊕
Tivoli Area

Copenhagen's veritable welcome mat, the Tivoli area is home to Central Station, the main tourist office and the city's most famous drawcard, Tivoli Gardens. Across the street from the gardens is Rådhuspladsen (City Hall Sq). Dominated by city hall (rådhus), this is the heart of Copenhagen. The square's design is inspired in part by the Palio, the famous piazza in Siena, Italy.

The Short List

○ **Tivoli Gardens (p40)** Indulge your inner kid in a vintage pleasure garden full of gleeful rides, storybook pavilions, live music and dance.

○ **Nationalmuseet (p44)** Eye up ancient bog bodies and Viking treasures on a trip through Danish history.

○ **Ny Carlsberg Glyptotek (p47)** Muse on Mediterranean antiquities, as well as French and Danish masterpieces, in a fabulously eclectic building.

○ **Rådhus (p47)** Hit Copenhagen's Tuscan-accented City Hall for its one-of-a-kind timepiece and dizzying rooftop views.

○ **Restaurant Mes (p48)** Book a table at one of the capital's most impressive contemporary restaurants.

Getting There & Around

🚌 Most city routes stop at Central Station or Rådhuspladsen. Take routes 6A and 26 for Frederiksberg Have via Vesterbro; route 1A for Slotsholmen, Nyhavn, the Royal Quarter and Østerbro; and routes 2A and 37 for Christianshavn.

🚈 All S-train lines stop at Central Station and Vesterport. Catch a Helsingør-bound regional train to Humlebæk for the Louisiana Museum of Modern Art.

Tivoli Area Map on p46

Fireworks over Tivolis Koncertsal (Concert Hall; p42)
TRABANTOS/SHUTTERSTOCK ©

Top Experience 📷

Enjoy Amusement Rides at Tivoli Gardens

Unleash your inner child at Tivoli Gardens. This veteran amusement park and pleasure garden has been eliciting gleeful shrills since 1843. It's the world's second-oldest amusement park, and one that inspired none other than Walt Disney. Generations on, the place continues to win fans with its dreamscape of rides, exotic pavilions, concerts, open-air stage shows and fireworks.

◉ MAP P46, A4

📞 33 15 10 01

www.tivoligardens.com

Vesterbrogade 3

adult/child 3-7yr 120/50kr, Fri after 7pm 175/100kr

🕐 11am-11pm Sun-Thu, to midnight Fri & Sat early Apr-late Sep, reduced hours rest of year

Star Flyer

One of the world's tallest carousels, the Star Flyer will have you whizzing round and round at heights of up to 80m. It's a bit like being on a skyscraping swing, travelling at 70km/h and taking in a breathtaking view of Copenhagen's historical towers and rooftops. The astrological symbols, quadrants and planets on the ride are a tribute of sorts to Danish astronomer Tycho Brahe.

Roller Coasters

Rutschebanen (The Roller Coaster) is the best loved of Tivoli's roller coasters, rollicking its way through and around a faux 'mountain' and reaching speeds of 60km/h. Built in 1914, it claims to be the world's oldest operating wooden roller coaster. If you're hankering for something a little more hardcore, jump on the Dæmonen (The Demon; pictured), a 21st-century beast with faster speeds and a trio of hair-raising loops.

Aquila

Like the Star Flyer, Aquila (Eagle) is also a nod to the country's most famous astronomer; the ride is named for the constellation that Brahe observed through his 16th-century telescope. The attraction itself is a breathtaking, gut-wrenching swing-and-spinner ride, with centrifugal powers up to 4G that will have you spinning around and upside down. If you enjoy viewing the world from a different angle, this one's for you...and your empty stomach.

The Grounds

Beyond the roller coasters, carousels and side stalls is a Tivoli of beautifully landscaped gardens, tranquil nooks and eclectic architecture. Lower the adrenaline under beautiful old chestnut and elm trees and amble around

★ Top Tips

○ Amusement-ride tickets cost 25kr (some rides require up to three tickets), making the unlimited-ride wristband (230kr) better value if you plan on staying a few hours.

○ Tivoli is at its most enchanting in the evening.

○ Although the free Friday music concerts (summer season only) commence at 10pm, head in by 8pm if it's a big-name act or risk missing out.

○ Lockers (small/large 30/50kr) are available on-site.

✕ Take a Break

Fill up on classic Danish fare at **Grøften** (☎ 33 75 06 75; www.groeften.dk; Tivoli Gardens, Vesterbrogade 3; smørrebrød 79-145kr; mains 149-385kr; ⏱ noon-10pm Sun-Thu, to 11pm Fri & Sat early Apr-late Sep, reduced hours rest of year; 🛜; 🚌 2A, 5C, 9A, 26, 250S, Ⓢ København H), Tivoli's most famous dining institution.

Tivoli Lake, gently rippling with koi carps, goldfish and ducks. Formed out of the old city moat, the lake is a top spot to snap pictures of Tivoli's commanding Chinese Tower, built in 1900. The lake itself is also home to the swashbuckling St George III, an 18th-century frigate turned restaurant.

Illuminations & Fireworks

Throughout the summer season, Tivoli Lake wows the crowds with its nightly laser and water spectacular. While it might not match the scale of similar shows in cities like Dubai and Las Vegas, its combination of lasers, shooting water and an orchestral score are still entertaining, especially with kids. The best spots to catch the show are from the bridge over Tivoli Lake or in the area in front of

the Vertigo ride. Another summer-season must are the Saturday-evening fireworks, repeated again from December 26 to 30 for Tivoli's annual Fireworks Festival. For a good view, make a beeline for Plænen (Tivoli's outdoor stage) or the area around the large fountain. For dates and times, see the website.

Live Performances

Tivoli delivers a jam-packed program of live music. The indoor Tivolis Koncertsal (Concert Hall) hosts mainly classical music, with the odd musical and big-name pop or rock act. Outdoor stage Plænen is the venue for Fredagsrock, Tivoli's free, hugely popular Friday-evening concerts. Running from mid-April to late September, the acts span numerous genres, from pop, rock

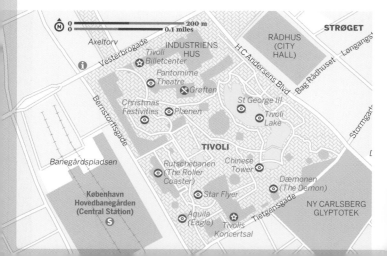

and neofolk, to hip-hop, jazz and funk (performers have included Lil Wayne, 5 Seconds of Summer and Erykah Badu). All tickets are sold at the Tivoli Billetcenter or online through the Tivoli website.

Christmas Festivities

Even the toughest scrooges find it hard not to melt at the sight of Tivoli in November and December, when the entire park turns into a Yuletide winter wonderland (cue live reindeer and special Christmas rides). The Tivoli Christmas market is one of the city's best-loved traditions, heady with the scent of cookies, pancakes and gløgg (mulled wine). It's also a good spot to pick up some nifty Nordic handicrafts.

Pantomime Theatre

Tivoli's criminally charming Pantomime Theatre debuted in 1874. It's the work of prolific architect Vilhelm Dahlerup, responsible for many of Copenhagen's most iconic buildings, including the Ny Carlsberg Glyptotek and Statens Museum for Kunst. Dahlerup's historicist style shines bright in his Tivoli creation, a colour-bursting ode to the Far East. While plays in the tradition of Italy's Commedia dell'arte are presented here, the stage also plays host to other styles of performances, including modern ballet. See the Tivoli website for details.

Top Experience 📷
Learn Danish History at Nationalmuseet

Copenhagen's National Museum hurls visitors through millennia of Danish history. Housed in a former royal palace, it's the country's veritable attic, with a hefty hoard that includes Denmark's fabled Sun Chariot, the well-preserved Huldremose Woman and revealing Viking artefacts. Beyond this is an eclectic mix of foreign acquisitions, including Chinese robes and Indigenous Australian objects.

⊙ MAP P46, D4

National Museum

📞 33 13 44 11

https://en.natmus.dk

Ny Vestergade 10

adult/child 95kr/free

🕙 10am-5pm Tue-Sun

🚌 1A, 2A, 9A, 12, 14, 26, 37,
Ⓜ Rådhuspladsen

Don't Miss

Danish Prehistory

Many of the museum's most spectacular finds are in the Prehistory Collection, located on the ground floor. Among these is a finely crafted 3500-year-old Sun Chariot and the spectacular Gundestrup cauldron (pictured), Europe's oldest example of Iron Age silverwork. Then there's the Huldremose Woman, a well-preserved Iron Age time traveller still wrapped in her cloaks.

Danish Middle Ages & Renaissance

The 1st floor harbours medieval and Renaissance objects from the period 1050 to 1660. Among them are *aquamaniles* (animal-shaped vessels used in Danish churches for hand-washing rituals). The most charming of these is a matching pair, consisting of a young man on horseback and the studiously indifferent woman he is attempting to woo. Both vessels narrowly escaped destruction when spotted on a conveyor belt at a quarry in Vigsø.

Stories of Denmark: 1660-2000

One floor up is the *Stories of Denmark: 1660–2000* exhibition, which traces Denmark's evolution from absolute monarchy to modern nation in three chronological sections: Under the Absolute Monarchy 1660–1848; People and Nation 1848–1915; and Welfare State 1915–2000. Topics include Denmark's string of humiliating wartime defeats, which forced this once powerful, conquering land to reassess its global role.

Ethnographic Treasures

The National Museum's ethnographic collection is one of its lesser-known fortes. Items include an extraordinary child's fur from Canada, fastened with 80 amulets, including fox teeth and a herring gull's foot. Such adornments were believed to ward off evil and lure good fortune.

★ Top Tips

○ Tickets are valid all day, allowing you to leave the museum and return later if you feel like breaking up your explorations. Free lockers are available.

○ The museum has a number of self-guided-tour brochures available for downloading on its website. Among these is a one-hour family tour as well as a children's guide to museum highlights.

✕ Take a Break

Skip the average museum restaurant for a classic Danish feast at nearby, canal-side Kanal Caféen (p48).

For a post-museum vino, kick back at Ved Stranden 10 (p57).

Tivoli Area Learn Danish History at Nationalmuseet

Ørsteds
Parken

Niels
Hemmingsensgade

Jamers
Plads

3

Vor Frue
Plads

Nørre Voldgade

Larsleijstræde

Sankt Peders Stræde

Studiestræde

Nørregade

Skindergade

Vimmelskaftet

H C Andersens Blvd

Vester Voldgade

Larsbjørnsstræde

6

Vestergade

Gammeltorv

Nygade

Hysterstræde

Snaregade

2

Frederiksberggade (Strøget)

Mikkel Bryggers
Gade

Nytorv

Knabrostræde

Kompagnistræde

Slotsholms Kanal
Vindebrogen

Rådhuspladsen

9

Heste-Gåsegade

Lavendelstræde

Rådhusstræde

Jernbanegade

Ⓜ

Rådhuspladsen

Farvergade

Løngangstræde

8

3

Axeltorv

Vesterbrogade

Industriens
Hus

2

Rådhus

Stormgade

Ny Vestergade

Frederiksholms Kanal

Nationalmuseet ◉

Frederiksholms Kanal

4

5

**Tivoli
Gardens**

TIVOLI

Dantes
Plads

Ny Kongensgade

4

Vester Voldgade

København
Hovedbanegården
(Central Station)

Ⓢ

Ny Carlsberg
Glyptotek

1

H C Andersens Blvd

7

Bernstorffsgade

Tietgensgade

Ved Glyptoteket

Hambrosgade

5

Christians Brygge

Mitchellsgade

6

For reviews see
- ◉ Top Experiences p40
- ◉ Sights p47
- ✕ Eating p48
- 🍷 Drinking p48
- ★ Entertainment p49

◭
Ⓝ
0 _____ 200 m
0 _____ 0.1 miles

Sydhavnen

A   B   C   D

Sights

Ny Carlsberg Glyptotek

MUSEUM

1 ◎ MAP P46, C4

Fin de siècle architecture meets with an eclectic mix of art at Ny Carlsberg Glyptotek. The collection is divided into two parts: Northern Europe's largest booty of antiquities, and an elegant collection of 19th-century Danish and French art. The latter includes the largest collection of Rodin sculptures outside of France and no less than 47 Gauguin paintings. These are displayed along with works by greats like Cézanne, Van Gogh, Pissarro, Monet and Renoir. (📞33 41 81 41; www.glyptoteket.com; Dantes Plads 7, HC Andersens Blvd; adult/

child 115kr/free, Tue free; ◎11am-6pm Tue, Wed & Fri-Sun, until 10pm Thu; 🚌1A, 2A, 9A, 37, Ⓜ Rådhuspladsen, Ⓢ København H)

Rådhus

HISTORIC BUILDING

2 ◎ MAP P46, B3

Completed in 1905, Copenhagen's national Romantic-style city hall is the work of architect Martin Nyrop. Inside is the curious **Jens Olsen's World Clock** (admission free; ◎9am-4pm Mon-Fri, 9.30am-1pm Sat), designed by astro mechanic Jens Olsen (1872–1945) and built at a cost of one million kroner. It displays not only local time, but also solar time, sidereal time, sunrises and sunsets, firmament and celestial-pole migration, planet revolutions, the Gregorian calen-

Jens Olsen's World Clock

TRABANTOS/SHUTTERSTOCK ©

Take a Break

Many visitors to Ny Carlsberg Glyptotek (p47) miss its wonderful rooftop terrace. Decked out with chairs for lazy lounging, it offers a breathtaking view of the museum's elegant dome, not to mention an impressive view over the city's spire-studded skyline. The rooftop is not accessible in inclement weather.

dar and even changing holidays! You can also climb the 105m city hall **tower** (30kr; ⏱tour 11am & 2pm Mon-Fri, noon Sat, minimum 4 people) for a commanding view. (City Hall; 📞33 66 25 86; www.kk.dk; Rådhuspladsen 1; admission free; ⏱9am-4pm Mon-Fri, 9.30am-1pm Sat; 🚌2A, 12, 14, 26, 33, 250S, Ⓢ København H)

Eating

Restaurant Mes   DANISH $$$

3 🍴 MAP P46, A1

Owned by chef Mads Rye Magnusson (former chef at Michelin-three-starred Geranium), this rising star is an intimate, refreshingly whimsical space, complete with moss feature wall and graffiti-soaked restrooms by local artist Fy. Most impressive is the menu, driven by market produce and the creative talent of its young head chef. (📞25 36 51 81; https://restaurant-mes.dk; Jarmers Plads 1; 5-course menu 350kr; ⏱5.30pm-

midnight Mon-Sat; 🛜; 🚌2A, 5C, 6A, 250S, Ⓢ Vesterport)

Kanal Caféen   DANISH $$

4 🍴 MAP P46, D4

Famed for its gruff staff and excellent herring, this cosy, nautically themed old-timer comes with a shaded summertime pontoon right on the canal. Order some Linie Aquavit (*snaps* matured at sea in oak-sherry casks) and the Kanal Platter, an epic, hunger-busting feast of Danish classics, including pickled herring, crumbed plaice, and roast pork with pickled red cabbage. (📞33 11 57 70; www.kanalcafeen.dk; Frederiksholms Kanal 18; smørrebrød 64-125kr, platters per person from 195kr; ⏱11am-5pm Mon-Fri, 11.30am-3pm Sat; 🚌1A, 2A, 9A, 14, 26, 37)

Drinking

Nimb Bar   COCKTAIL BAR

5 🍷 MAP P46, A4

If you have a weakness for crystal chandeliers (the originals from 1909), quirky murals and an open fire with your well-mixed drink, make sure this ballroom bar is on your list. Located inside super-chic Hotel Nimb, it was founded by legendary bartender Angus Winchester. The beer is expensive, but you're here for seasonal, classically styled cocktails. Period. (📞88 70 00 00; www.nimb.dk; Hotel Nimb, Bernstorffsgade 5; ⏱11am-midnight Sun-Thu, to 1am Fri & Sat; 🛜; 🚌2A, 5C, 9A, 26, 66, 250S, Ⓢ København H)

Living Room
CAFE

6 😊 MAP P46, B2

Spread over three levels and decked out in vintage decor and a Moroccan-themed tea room, the aptly titled Living Room is a super-cosy (albeit often busy) spot to settle in with a speciality coffee, tea, homemade smoothie or lemonade. Cocktails and other alcoholic libations are also served late into the evening. (📞33 32 66 10; www.facebook.com/thelivingroom dk; Larsbjørnsstræde 17; ⏰9am-11pm Mon-Thu, to 2am Fri, 10am-2am Sat, 10am-7pm Sun; 🛜; 🚌5C, 6A, 10, 14, Ⓜ️Nørreport, Ⓢ Nørreport)

Entertainment

Tivoli Koncertsal
CONCERT VENUE

7 😊 MAP P46, B5

The Tivoli concert hall hosts Danish and international symphony orchestras, string quartets and other classical-music performances, not to mention contemporary music artists and dance companies. Purchase tickets online or at the Tivoli Box Office by the main Tivoli Gardens entrance on Vesterbrogade. (Concert Hall; www.tivoligardens.

com; Tietgensgade 30; 🚌1A, 2A, 5C, 9A, 37, 250S, Ⓢ København H)

Mojo
BLUES

8 😊 MAP P46, C3

East of Tivoli, this is a great spot for deep, soulful blues and its associated genres, from bluegrass and zydeco to soul. There are live acts nightly, followed by DJ-spun tunes. The vibe is warm, convivial and relaxed, and there's draught beer aplenty. (📞33 11 64 53; www.mojo.dk; Løngangstræde 21C; ⏰8pm-5am; 🚌1A, 2A, 9A, 12, 14, 26, 33, 37, Ⓢ København H)

Grand Teatret
CINEMA

9 😊 MAP P46, B3

Just off Strøget, this historic theatre from 1923 screens a range of films from European art-house productions to mainstream dramas. You won't find popcorn here – the on-site cafe serves simple bites like quiche and cake, as well as organic, fair-trade coffee and top-notch teas.

English-language films are presented with Danish subtitles. (📞33 15 16 11; www.grandteatret.dk; Mikkel Bryggers Gade 8; ⏰9am-10.30pm; 🛜; 🚌12, 14, 26, 33, Ⓢ København H)

Explore ◉
Slotsholmen

Slotsholmen is a spire-spiked island heaving with history. At its heart is Christiansborg Slot, home to the national government. Beneath it lie traces of Copenhagen's medieval past, while around it there is an abundance of museums including the Thorvaldsens Museum, an ode to Denmark's greatest sculptor. Adding sharp relief is the Royal Library's 'Black Diamond', one of Scandinavia's most applauded contemporary buildings.

The Short List

○ **Christiansborg Slot (p52)** *Explore lavish interiors, innovative tapestries and original fortress ruins in Denmark's house of power.*

○ **Thorvaldsens Museum (p59)** *Spend quiet time among the works and collectables of the great Danish sculptor Bertel Thorvaldsen.*

○ **Det Kongelige Bibliotek (p59)** *Take in the monumental harbour view from Copenhagen's Royal Library, a masterpiece of Nordic architecture.*

○ **Dansk Arkitektur Center (p59)** *Find urban enlightenment inside starchitect Rem Koolhaas' innovative Blox building.*

○ **Tårnet (p61)** *Savour polished takes on classic Nordic flavours in the Danish Parliament's landmark tower.*

Getting There & Around

🚌 Slotsholmen is well serviced by bus, with routes 1A, 2A, 9A, 14, 26, 37 and 66 all running across the island. Slotsholmen itself is easily navigable on foot.

Ⓜ The closest metro station is Christianshavn, 400m east of Slotsholmen.

⚓ Commuter ferries stop just beside Det Kongelige Bibliotek.

Slotsholmen Map on p58

Det Kongelige Bibliotek (p59)
ARCHITECTS: SCHMIDT HAMMER LASSEN; IMAGE: KATEAFTER/SHUTTERSTOCK ©

Top Experience

See the Ruins of Christiansborg Slot

Fans of the Danish political drama Borgen will know it as the workplace of statsminister Birgitte Nyborg. Others will know it as that slightly foreboding palace in the heart of Copenhagen. This is Denmark's power base, home to the Danish parliament, Prime Minister's office and Supreme Court, not to mention an eclectic array of cultural draws, from tapestries to carriages.

◉ MAP P58, B2

Christiansborg Palace

☎ 33 92 64 92

www.christiansborg.dk

Prins Jørgens Gård 1

adult/child 150kr/free

🕒 9am-5pm, closed Mon Oct-Apr

🚌 1A, 2A, 9A, 26, 37, 66,

🚇 Det Kongelige Bibliotek

Royal Reception Rooms

The grandest part of Christiansborg is **De Kongelige Repræsentationslokaler** (Royal Reception Rooms at Christiansborg Slot; www.christiansborg.dk; Slotsholmen; adult/child 90kr/free; ⏰9am-5pm, closed Mon Oct-Apr; 🚌1A, 2A, 9A, 26, 37, 66, 🚢Det Kongelige Bibliotek, Ⓜ️Gammel Strand; pictured), a series of 18 elegant palace rooms and halls used by the queen to hold royal banquets and entertain heads of state. The Queen's Library is especially memorable; a gilded wonderland adorned with dripping chandeliers, ornate stucco, ceiling storks and a small part of the royal family's centuries-old book collection. Top billing, however, goes to the sweeping Great Hall, home to riotously colourful wall tapestries depicting 1000 years of Danish history. Created by tapestry designer Bjørn Nørgaard over a decade, the works were completed in 2000. Keep an eye out for the Adam and Eve–style representation of the queen and her husband (albeit clothed) in a Danish Garden of Eden.

Fortress Ruins

A walk through the crypt-like bowels of Slotsholmen, known as **Ruinerne under Christiansborg** (Ruins under Christiansborg; adult/child 50kr/free; ⏰10am-5pm, closed Mon Oct-Apr; 🚌1A, 2A, 9A, 26, 37, 66, 🚢Det Kongelige Bibliotek, Ⓜ️Gammel Strand), offers a unique perspective on Copenhagen's well-seasoned history. In the basement of the current palace are the ruins of Slotsholmen's original fortress – built by Bishop Absalon in 1167 – and its successor, Copenhagen Castle. Among these remnants are each building's ring walls, plus a well, baking oven, sewer drains and stonework from the castle's Blue Tower. The tower is infamously remembered as the place in which Christian IV's daughter, Leonora Christina, was incarcerated for treason from 1663 to 1685.

★ Top Tips

o If you plan on visiting several of the sights at Christiansborg Slot, opt for the combination ticket. Costing 150kr (children aged under 18 enter free of charge), it includes access to the Royal Reception Rooms, the Fortress Ruins, the Royal Stables, as well as the surprisingly interesting Royal Kitchen. The ticket is valid for one month.

✗ Take a Break

o Book a lunch table at Tårnet (p61) for exceptional smørre-brød, beers and a view of Tivoli.

Royal Stables

Completed in 1740, the two curved, symmetrical wings behind Christiansborg Slot belonged to the original baroque palace, destroyed by fire in 1794. The wings still house De Kongelige Stalde (p60) and its museum of antique coaches, uniforms and riding paraphernalia, some of which are used for royal receptions. Among these is the 19th-century Gold Coach, adorned with 24-karat gold leaf and used by the royal couple on their gallop from Amalienborg to Christiansborg during the New Year's levee in January.

The Tower

The **palace tower** (https://taarnet.dk; ⊘11am-9pm Tue-Sun; 🚌1A, 2A, 9A, 26, 37, 66, 📖Det Kongelige Bibliotek, Ⓜ Christianshavn) opened to the public for the first time in 2014. It's the city's tallest tower, delivering a sweeping view over the Danish capital. The tower is also home to Tårnet (p61), a restaurant owned by prolific restaurateur Rasmus Bo Bojesen. Lunch features contemporary smørrebrød (open sandwiches) and Danish cheeses; and is a better bet than the dinner, both in terms of value and the view. It's a popular nosh spot, so book ahead if you plan on staking out a table.

Christiansborg Slotskirke

Tragedy struck CF Hansen's austere, 19th-century neoclassical **Christiansborg Slotskirke** (⊘10am-5pm Sun, daily Jul; 🚌1A, 2A, 9A, 26, 37, 66) on the day of the 1992 Copenhagen Carnival. A stray firework hit the scaffolding that had surrounded the church during a lengthy restoration and set the roof ablaze, destroying the dome. With no surviving architectural plans of the dome and roof construction to consult, architectural archaeologists systematically recorded all the charred remains before painstakingly reconstructing the chapel. Miraculously, a remarkable frieze by Bertel Thorvaldsen that rings the ceiling just below the dome survived.

Theatre Museum

Dating from 1767, the wonderfully atmospheric Hofteater (Old Court Theatre) has hosted everything from Italian opera to local ballet troupes, one of which included fledgling ballet student Hans Christian Andersen. Taking its current appearance in 1842, the venue is now the **Teatermuseet** (Theatre Museum; 📞33 11 51 76; www.teatermuseet.dk; Christiansborg Ridebane 18; adult/child 40kr/free; ⊘noon-4pm Tue-Sun; 🚌1A, 2A, 9A, 26, 37, 66), and visitors are free to explore the stage, boxes and dressing rooms, along with displays of set models, drawings, costumes and period posters tracing the history of Danish theatre.

Christiansborg Slot's History

Christiansborg Slot is an architectural phoenix. The current palace is simply the latest in a series of buildings to have graced the site, among them medieval castles and an elegant baroque beauty.

Bishop Absalon's Castle

According to medieval chronicler Saxo Grammaticus, Bishop Absalon of Roskilde built a castle on a small islet in the waters off the small town of Havn. The islet would become Slotsholmen. Erected in 1167 the castle was encircled by a limestone curtain wall, the ruins of which can still be seen today under the current complex. Despite frequent attacks, Absalon's creation stood strong for two centuries until a conflict between Valdemar IV of Denmark and the Hanseatic League saw the latter tear it down in 1369.

Copenhagen Castle

By the end of the 14th century, the site was once again thriving, this time as the address of Copenhagen Castle. The new, improved model came with a moat, as well as a solid, towered entrance. The castle remained the property of the Bishop of Roskilde until 1417, when Erik of Pomerania seized control, turning the castle into a royal abode. Nipped and tucked over time – Christian IV added a spire to the entrance tower – the castle was completely rebuilt by Frederik IV, evidently with dubious engineering advice. The castle began to crack under its own weight, leading to its hasty demolition in the 1730s.

Christiansborg: One, Two, Three

The demolition led to the debut of the first Christiansborg Slot in 1745. Commissioned by Christian VI and designed by architect Elias David Häusser, it went up in flames in 1794, its only surviving remnant being the Royal Riding Complex, home to the Royal Stables. Rebuilt in the early 19th century, it became the seat of parliament in 1849 before once more succumbing to fire in 1884. In 1907 the cornerstone for the third Christiansborg Slot was laid by Frederik VIII. Designed by Thorvald Jørgensen and completed in 1928, it's a truly national affair, its neo-baroque facade adorned with granite sourced from across the country.

Walking Tour 🥾

A Slotsholmen Saunter

Looks can be very deceiving. While Slotsholmen may look small on a city map, this compact island is Denmark's powerhouse. It's right here that politicians debate policy, that supreme court judges set precedents, and that the Queen plays host with the most. This easy meander will have you crossing Copenhagen's most romantic bridge, scanning the city from its tallest tower and relaxing in a harbour turned secret library garden.

Walk Facts

Start Marmorbroen;
Bus: 1A, 2A, 9A, 26, 37 to
Stormbroen.

End Ved Stranded 10 (bus)
1A, 2A, 9A, 26, 37 to Christiansborg Slotsplads

Length 2km; 1.5 hours

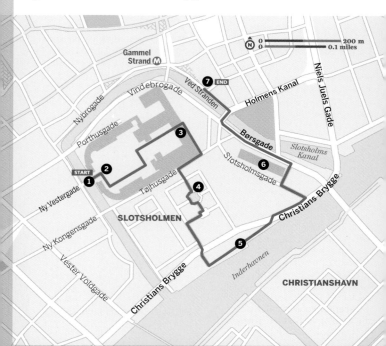

❶ Marmorbroen

Designed by Nicolai Eigtved, the **Marble Bridge** is one of Copenhagen's rococo highlights. Completed in 1745, it dates from the original Christiansborg Slot, which went up in flames in 1794.

❷ Christiansborg Ridebane

The **Riding Ground complex** also survived the fire, offering a glimpse of the palace's original baroque style. The square's only decoration is Vilhelm Bissen's 19th-century equestrian statue of Frederik VII.

❸ Christiansborg Slot Tower

Head into Christiansborg Slot through the main entrance to climb the palace **tower** (p54). Fans of the Danish TV drama Borgen will know that it's right here that Birgitte's mentor Bent Sejrø encourages her to fight for the role of statsminister.

❹ Det Kongelige Biblioteks Have

The open archways of the red-brick building facing Christiansborg Slot's southern side lead to the charming **Royal Library Garden**. The garden sits on Christian IV's old naval port, Tøjhushavnen. The towering fountain sculpture is an ode to the written word. Created by Mogens Møller, it shoots out water every hour on the hour. Look out for the 1918 bronze statue of 19th-century philosopher, poet and theologian Søren Kierkegaard by sculptor Louis Hasselriis.

❺ Det Kongelige Bibliotek

Just south of the garden, **Det Kongelige Bibliotek** (p59) is home to the **Black Diamond**, the library's world-renowned extension. Completed in 1999, the building's sleek, somber facade is clad in black granite sourced from Zimbabwe and polished in Italy. Head to the upper floors for a spectacular view of the atrium.

❻ Børsen

Head north along the waterfront, then turn left onto Slotsholmsgade to reach 17th-century **Børsen** (p59). Copenhagen's old stock exchange, it was originally flanked by water on three sides and topped with a lead roof. The lead was used to make cannonballs during the Swedish occupation in 1658–59.

❼ Ved Stranden 10

From Børsen, cross Holmens Bro and treat yourself to a well-earned tipple at **Ved Stranden 10**, a well-versed wine bar with canalside seating in the summer and snug, Danish designer interiors.

✗ Take a Break

Sip and graze at one of Copenhagen's best wine bars, **Ved Stranden 10** (☎ 35 42 40 40; www.vedstranden10.dk; Ved Stranden 10; ☉ noon-10pm Mon-Sat; 🚍1A, 2A, 9A, 26, 37, 66, 350S).

CHRISTIANSHAVN

Niels Juels Gade

Nationalbanken

Christian IV's Bro

Knippelsbro

Havnegade

Havnegade

Holmens Kanal

Nikolajgade

Laksegade

Admiralgade

Slotsholms Kanal

Børsgade

Børsen ⊙ 3

Slotsholmsgade

Ministerialbygning

Christians Brygge

Inderhavnen

Søren Kierkegaards Plads

✕ 8

Ved Stranden

Holmens Bro

Det Kongelige Bibliotek ⊙ 2

Det Kongelige Biblioteks Have

⊙

Dansk Jødisk Museum 4 ⊙

Højbro

Vindebrogade

Christiansborg Slotsplads

Tøjhusgade

✕ 7

SLOTSHOLMEN

Christiansborg Slot ⊙

Tøjhusmuseet ⊙ 6

Christian IV's Bryghus

Bertel Thorvaldsens Plads

1 Thorvaldsens ⊙ Museum

Christiansborg Ridebane

De Kongelige Stalde ⊙ 5

Prinsensbro

Marmorbroen

Frederiksholms Kanal

Portugalsgade

Stormbro

Frederiksholms Kanal

Slotsholms Kanal

Snaregade

Knabrostræde

Magstræde

Nybrogade

Nationalmuseet

Nyhavnsgade

100 m
0.05 miles

N

For reviews see	
⊙ Top Experiences	p52
⊙ Sights	p59
✕ Eating	p61

Sights

Thorvaldsens Museum
MUSEUM

1 MAP P58, B1

What looks like a colourful Greco-Roman mausoleum is in fact a museum dedicated to the works of illustrious Danish sculptor Bertel Thorvaldsen (1770–1844). Heavily influenced by mythology after four decades in Rome, Thorvaldsen returned to Copenhagen and donated his private collection to the Danish public. In return the royal family provided this site for the construction of what is a remarkable complex housing Thorvaldsen's drawings, plaster moulds and statues. The museum also contains Thorvaldsen's own collection of Mediterranean antiquities. (📞33 32 15 32; www.thorvaldsensmuseum.dk; Bertel Thorvaldsens Plads 2; adult/child 70kr/free, Wed free; ⏰10am-5pm Tue-Sun; 🚌1A, 2A, 26, 37, 66, Ⓜ Gammel Strand)

Det Kongelige Bibliotek
LIBRARY

2 MAP P58, D4

Scandinavia's largest library consists of two very distinct parts: the original 19th-century red-brick building and the head-turning 'Black Diamond' extension, the latter a leaning parallelogram of sleek black granite and smoke-coloured glass. From the soaring, harbour-fronting atrium, an escalator leads up to a 210 sq metre ceiling mural by celebrated Danish artist Per Kirkeby. Beyond it, at the end of the corridor, is the 'old library' and its Hogwarts-like northern Reading Room, resplendent with vintage desk lamps and classical columns. (Royal Library; 📞33 47 47 47; www.kb.dk; Søren Kierkegaards Plads; admission free; ⏰8am-7pm Mon-Fri, from 9am Sat Jul & Aug, 8am-9pm Mon-Fri, 9am-7pm Sat rest of year; 🚌66, 🚇Det Kongelige Bibliotek)

Børsen
HISTORIC BUILDING

3 MAP P58, E2

Not many stock exchanges are topped by a 56m-tall spire formed from the entwined tails of four

Architecture Exhibitions

Located inside architect Rem Koolhaas' harbourside Blox building, the **Dansk Arkitektur Center** (Dansk Arkitektur Center; 📞Danish Architecture Centre; DAC; exhibition adult/child 60kr/free, 5-9pm Wed free; ⏰exhibition & bookshop 10am-5pm Mon, Tue & Thu-Sun, to 9pm Wed, cafe from 10am Mon-Fri, 10am-4:30pm Sat & Sun; Ⓜ Christianshavn, 🚌Christianshavn) hosts changing exhibitions on Danish and international architecture, and houses an excellent book- and designshop. On weekends DAC also runs 90-minute walking tours of the city's contemporary architecture (125kr). See the website for details.

dragons. Børsen is one. Constructed in the bustling early-17th-century reign of Christian IV, the building is considered one of the finest examples of Dutch Renaissance architecture in Denmark, with richly embellished gables. Its still-functioning chamber of commerce is the oldest in Europe, though the building is not generally open to the public. (Børsgade; 🚌2A, 9A, 37, 66)

Dansk Jødisk Museum MUSEUM

4 ◉ MAP P58, D4

Designed by Polish-born Daniel Libeskind, the Danish Jewish Museum occupies the former Royal Boat House, an early-17th-century building once part of Christian IV's harbour complex. The transformed interior is an intriguing geometrical space, home to a permanent exhibition documenting Danish Jewry. Historical events covered include the Rescue of the Danish Jews in WWII, in which most of the country's Jewish population managed to flee to neutral Sweden with the help of the Danish resistance movement and ordinary Danish citizens. (📞33 11 22 18; www.jewmus.dk; Proviantpassagen 6, Kongelige Bibliotekshave (Royal Library Garden); adult/child 60kr/free; ⏰10am-5pm Tue-Sun Jun-Aug, 1-4pm Tue-Fri, noon-5pm Sat & Sun rest of the year; 🚌66, 🛥Det Kongelige Bibliotek)

De Kongelige Stalde MUSEUM

5 ◉ MAP P58, B3

Completed in 1740, the two curved, symmetrical wings behind Christiansborg belonged to the original baroque palace, destroyed by fire in 1794. The wings still house the royal stables and its museum of antique coaches, uniforms and riding paraphernalia, some of which are used for royal receptions. Among these is the 19th-century Gold Coach, adorned with 24-carat gold leaf and still used by the queen on her gallop from Amalienborg to Christiansborg during the New Year's levee in January. (Royal Stables; 📞33 40 10 10; www.kongehuset.dk; adult/child 50kr/free; ⏰1.30-4pm daily May-Sep, closed Mon Oct-Apr, guided tours in English 2pm Sat; 🚌1A, 2A, 9A, 26, 37, 66)

Dansk Jødisk Museum

Tøjhusmuseet MUSEUM

6 ⊙ MAP P58, C3

The Royal Arsenal Museum houses an impressive collection of historic weaponry, from canons and medieval armour to pistols, swords and even a WWII flying bomb. Built by Christian IV in 1600, the 163m-long building is Europe's longest vaulted Renaissance hall. (Royal Danish Arsenal Museum; ☎33 11 60 37; www.natmus.dk; Tøjhusgade 3; adult/child 65kr/free; ⊙10am-5pm Tue-Sun; 🚌1A, 2A, 9A, 14, 26, 37, 66)

Eating

Tårnet DANISH $$

7 ✖ MAP P58, C2

Book ahead for lunch at Tårnet, owned by prolific restaurateur Rasmus Bo Bojesen and memorably set inside Christiansborg Slot's commanding tower. Lunch here is better value than dinner, with superlative, contemporary smørrebrød that is among the city's best. While the general guideline is two smørrebrød per person, some of the à la carte versions are quite substantial (especially the tartare), so check before ordering. (☎33 37 31 00; http://taarnet.dk/restauranten; Christiansborg Slotsplads, Christiansborg Slot; lunch smørrebrød 85-135kr, dinner mains 235kr; ⊙11.30am-11pm Tue-Sun, kitchen closes 10pm; 🛜; 🚌1A, 2A, 9A, 26, 37, 66, 🕱Det Kongelige Bibliotek)

Music at One

If possible, drop into the Black Diamond at the **Royal Library** (p59) at 1pm, when the usually quiet space breaks into a dramatic, three-minute soundscape. Created by Danish composer Jens Vilhelm Pedersen (aka Fuzzy) and titled *Katalog* (Catalogue), the work consists of 52 individual electro-acoustic compositions, one for each week of the year.

Søren K NEW NORDIC $$$

8 ✖ MAP P58, D4

Bathed in light on even the dourest of days, the Royal Library's crisp, harbourfront fine-diner revels in flaunting top-notch, seasonal ingredients. The menu focuses on small plates, each delivering delicate, contemporary takes on mainly Nordic flavours, whether it be raw scallop with salted cucumber and green tomato bouillon, or Norwegian lobster with anchovy and kale. Come for the quality, not the portions. (☎33 47 49 49; http://soerenk.dk; Søren Kierkegaards Plads 1; 1/5 courses 120/500kr; ⊙noon-3pm & 5.30-10pm Mon-Sat; 🛜; 🚌66, 🕱Det Kongelige Bibliotek)

Explore

Strøget & Around

Pedestrianised Strøget (pronounced 'stroll') weaves through Copenhagen's historical core from Rådhuspladsen to Kongens Nytorv. Many of the most interesting sights, restaurants, bars and boutiques, however, lie off the main drag, in or around the old Latin Quarter. Among them is Copenhagen's austere, sculpture-graced cathedral and King Christian IV's curious 17th-century Round Tower.

The Short List

○ **Latin Quarter (p66)** Wander cobbled streets and photogenic squares in Copenhagen's cosiest historic district.

○ **Rundetårn (p66)** Follow in the footsteps of mighty kings and astronomers for breathtaking views of the Danish capital.

○ **Vor Frue Kirke (p66)** Admire Bertel Thorvaldsen's most famous sculptures in a cathedral fit for royal weddings.

○ **Schønnemann (p68)** Feast on Denmark's finest smørrebrød (open sandwiches) at a time-warped, 19th-century favourite.

○ **Hay House (p73)** Restyle your home with coveted items from some of the world's hottest independent designers.

Getting There & Around

🚌 Most major routes skirt the compact historic centre. The only route that actually traverses it is route 14, connecting Nørreport to Vesterbro via Tivoli Gardens and Central Station.

Ⓜ Kongens Nytorv station is just off the eastern end of Strøget. At the northwest edge of the city centre lies Nørreport station, serving both the metro and S-train.

Strøget & Around Map on p64

For reviews see

◉	Sights	p66
✖	Eating	p68
☕	Drinking	p69
☆	Entertainment	p71
🔒	Shopping	p73

0 — 200 m
0 — 0.1 miles

Nørreport Ⓜ

Nørreport Ⓢ

Vendersgade

Linnésgade

Israels Plads

Frederiksborggade

Rosenborggade

Hausergade

Kultorvet

Rosengården

Nørre Voldgade

Nørregade

Flstræde

Peder Hvitfeldts Stræde

Rosengården

Ørsteds Parken

Krystalgade

Larslejsstræde

Teglgårdsstræde

1 ◉   ☕16

Latin Quarter

Københavns Universitet

Kannikestræde

Klosterstræde

Vor Frue Plads

◉3

Vor Frue Kirke

Skindergade

Skoubogade

11 ✖

Sankt Pedersstræde

Larsbjørnsstræde

Studiestræde

Gammeltorv

Nygade

Nytorv

Brolæggerstræde

Studiestræde

Vester Voldgade

Vestergade

Frederiksberggade (Strøget)

Kattesundet

Sluttergade

Knabrostræde

Heste-Gæsgade

Kompagnistræde

Rådhustræde

H C Andersens Blvd

Jernbanegade

Ⓜ Rådhuspladsen

Rådhuspladsen

Lavendelstræde

Regnbuepladsen

Farvergade

Løngangstræde

Vesterbrogade

Tivoli

Rådhus (City Hall)

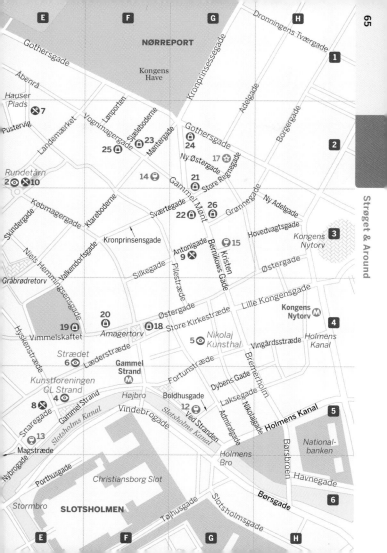

E

F

G

H

Dronningens Tværgade

1

Gothersgade

NØRREPORT

Kongens
Have

Kronprinsessegade

Adelgade

Borgergade

Åbenrå

Hauser
Plads

7

Pustervig

Landemærket

Lønporten

Vognmagergade

Skæleboderne

Møntergade

23

25

Gothersgade

24

Ny Østergade

17

Ny Østergade

Store Regnegade

2

Rundetårn

2   10

Købmagergade

Klareboderne

14

Gammel Mønt

21

26

22

Grønnegade

Ny Adelgade

Skindergade

Niels Hemmingsensgade

Valkendorfsgade

Kronprinsensgade

Sværtegade

Antonigade

9

Bernikows Gade

Pilestræde

15

Kristen

Hovedvagtsgade

Kongens
Nytorv

3

Østergade

Gråbrødretorv

Silkegade

Østergade

Store Kirkestræde

Lille Kongensgade

Kongens
Nytorv

4

Hyskenstræde

19

Vimmelskaftet

20

Amagertorv

18

Nikolaj
Kunsthal

5

Vingårdsstræde

Holmens
Kanal

Strædet

6

Læderstræde

Fortunstræde

Bremerholm

Kunstforeningen
GL Strand

4

Gammel
Strand

Dybens Gade

Nikolajgade

8

Snaregade

Gammel Strand

Højbro

Boldhusgade

12

Laksegade

Admiralgade

Holmens Kanal

5

13

Slotsholms Kanal

Vindebrogade

Ved Stranden

Slotsholms Kanal

Holmens Kanal

Magstræde

Holmens
Bro

Børsbroen

National-
banken

Nybrogade

Porthusgade

Christiansborg Slot

Havnegade

Stormbro

SLOTSHOLMEN

Tøjhusgade

Slotsholmsgade

Børsgade

Børsgade

6

E

F

G

H

Sights

Latin Quarter

AREA

1 MAP P64, D3

Bordered by Nørre Voldgade to the north, Nørregade to the east, Vestergade to the south and Vester Voldgade to the west, the Latin Quarter gets its nickname from the presence of the old campus of **Københavns Universitet** (Copenhagen University), where Latin was once widely spoken. This is one of Copenhagen's oldest and most atmospheric districts, dotted with historic, pastel-hued buildings and postcard-pretty nooks. Among the latter is **Gråbrødretorv** (Grey Friars' Square), which dates from the mid-17th century. (5C, 6A, 14, Nørreport, Nørreport)

Rundetårn

HISTORIC BUILDING

2 MAP P64, E2

Haul yourself to the top of the 34.8m-high red-brick 'Round Tower' and you will be following in the footsteps of such luminaries as King Christian IV, who built it in 1642 as an astronomical observatory as well as a tower for the new university church, Trinitatis. You'll also be following in the hoofsteps of Tsar Peter the Great's horse and, according to legend, the track marks of a car that made its way up the tower's spiral ramp in 1902. (Round Tower; 33 73 03 73; www.rundetaarn.dk; Købmagergade 52; adult/child 25/5kr; 10am-8pm May-Sep, reduced hours rest of year,

observatory times vary; ; 14, Nørreport, Nørreport)

Vor Frue Kirke

CATHEDRAL

3 MAP P64, D4

Founded in 1191 and rebuilt three times after devastating fires, Copenhagen's neoclassical cathedral dates from 1829. Designed by CF Hansen, its lofty, vaulted interior houses Bertel Thorvaldsen's statues of Christ and the apostles, completed in 1839 and considered his most acclaimed works. In fact, the sculptor's depiction of Christ, with comforting open arms, remains the most popular worldwide model for statues of Jesus. In May 2004, the cathedral hosted the wedding of Crown Prince Frederik to Australian Mary Donaldson. (33 15 10 78; www.koebenhavnsdomkirke.dk; Nørregade 8; 8am-5pm, closed during services & concerts; 14, Nørreport, Nørreport)

Kunstforeningen GL Strand

GALLERY

4 MAP P64, E5

The HQ of Denmark's artists' union continues to foster emerging and forward-thinking talent with around six to eight exhibitions of modern and contemporary art each year. The work of both Danish and international artists is explored, with an underlying emphasis on current and emerging trends in the art world. That said, retrospectives are also occasionally offered; a recent exhibition showcased the work of Finnish illustrator and writer Tove Jansson, creator of the much-loved Moomins storybook characters. (📞33 36 02 60; www.glstrand.dk; Gammel Strand 48; adult/child 75kr/free; 🕐11am-5pm Tue & Thu-Sun, to 8pm Wed; 🚇1A, 2A, 9A, 26, 37, 66, Ⓜ Kongens Nytorv)

Nikolaj Kunsthal
GALLERY

5 ◎ MAP P64, G4

Built in the 13th century, the church of Sankt Nikolaj is now home to the **Copenhagen Contemporary Art Centre**, which hosts around half a dozen exhibitions annually. Exhibitions tend to focus on modern-day cultural, political and social issues, explored in mediums as diverse as photography and performance art. The centre also houses a snug, well-regarded Danish restaurant called **Maven**. (📞33 18 17 80; www.nikolajkunsthal.dk; Nikolaj Plads 10; adult/child 60kr/free, Wed free; 🕐noon-6pm Tue-Fri, 11am-5pm Sat & Sun; 🚇1A, 2A, 9A, 26, 37, 66, 350S, Ⓜ Kongens Nytorv)

Strædet
STREET

6 ◎ MAP P64, E4

Running parallel to crowded Strøget, Strædet is technically made up of two streets, Kompagnistræde and Læderstræde. The strip is a good spot to shop for local ceramics and antiques, though its cafes are mostly mediocre. Many of Strædet's medieval and Renaissance-era buildings were destroyed in the great fire of 1795, though some do survive. These

Gråbrødretorv

Smart Bikes

Copenhagen's bike-share is called **Bycyklen** (City Bikes; www.bycyklen.dk; per hr 30kr). Available 24/7, 365 days a year, these 'Smart Bikes' feature touchscreen tablets with GPS, electric motors, puncture-resistant tyres and locks. The bikes can be accessed from a large number of docking stations dotted across the city, including at Central Station, Vesterport, Østerport and Dybbølsbro S-train stations. To use, you will first need to create an account on the Bycyklen website. Check the website for docking stations locations and real-time bicycle availability at each. Rental itself costs 30kr per hour.

include the buildings at numbers 23, 25, 31 and 33, all of which date back to the first half of the 1700s. (🚌1A, 2A,9A, 14, 26, 37, 66)

Eating

Schønnemann   DANISH $$

7 🍴 MAP P64, E2

A veritable institution, Schønnemann has been lining bellies with smørrebrød and *snaps* since 1877. Originally a hit with farmers in town selling their produce, the restaurant's current fan base includes revered chefs like René Redzepi; try the smørrebrød named after

him: smoked halibut with creamed cucumber, radishes and chives on caraway bread. (📞33 12 07 85; www.restaurantschonnemann.dk; Hauser Plads 16; smørrebrød 75-185kr; 🕙11.30am-5pm Mon-Sat; 📶; 🚌6A, 42, 150S, 184, 185, 🅼Nørreport, 🆂Nørreport)

Marv & Ben   NEW NORDIC $$$

8 🍴 MAP P64, E5

Cellar restaurant 'Marrow & Bone' has been repeatedly awarded a Michelin Bib Gourmand in recognition of its value for money. Its New Nordic menu can be approached in various ways: a la carte or as four- or six-course tasting menus. Dishes are imaginative and evocative, celebrating Nordic landscapes and moods in creations like hay-smoked mackerel with chamomile, or squid with kelp and buttermilk. (📞33 91 01 91; www.marvogben.dk; Snaregade 4; small dishes 85-135kr, 4-/6-course menu 400/600kr; 🕙5.30pm-1am Tue-Sat; 📶; 🚌1A, 2A, 9A, 14, 26, 37)

The Market   ASIAN $$

9 🍴 MAP P64, G3

Dark, svelte and contemporary (we love the dramatically back-lit bar and organically shaped crockery), The Market pumps out vibrant pan-Asian dishes like delicate brown-crab salad with apple, dashi and avocado, or expertly grilled poussin dressed in coconut sauce and fresh mango slithers. The sushi is commendable, particularly the maki. Book ahead, especially if dining on a Friday or Saturday night. (📞70 70 24 35; http://the marketcph.dk; Antonigade 2; mains 155-350kr, 12-course menu 595kr; 🕐11.30am-4pm & 5-10pm Mon-Thu, to 10.30am Fri & Sat, to 9.30pm Sun; 🚇1A, 26, Ⓜ Kongens Nytorv)

DØP
HOT DOGS $

10 🍴 MAP P64, E2

Danes love a good *pølse* (sausage), and hot-dog vans are ubiquitous across Copenhagen. DØP is the best, with a van right beside Rundetårn (Round Tower). Everything here is organic, from the meat and vegetables to the toppings. Options range from a classic Danish roasted hot dog with mustard, ketchup, remoulade, pickles and onions both fresh and fried, to a new-school vegan tofu version. (📞30 20 40 25; www.døp.dk; Købmagergade 50; hot dogs from 35kr; 🕐10:30am-6:30pm Mon-Thurs, til 7pm Fri, 10:30am-6:30pm Sat; 🚻; 🚇6A, 5C, Ⓜ Nørreport, Ⓢ Nørreport)

La Glace
BAKERY $

11 🍴 MAP P64, D4

Copenhagen's oldest *konditori* (pastry shop) has been compromising waistlines since 1870. Slip into its maze of time-warped rooms and succumb to a slice of the classic *valnøddekage* (walnut cake), a cheeky combo of crushed and caramelised walnuts, whipped cream and mocca glacé. If you're a marzipan lover, opt for the chocolate-covered Dachstein; its moist, flavourful centre is good

Hearty Meals

Cosy, creaky, wood-panelled **Café Halvvejen** (📞33 11 91 12; www.cafehalvvejen.dk; Krystalgade 11; dishes 59-175kr; 🕐11am-2am Mon-Thu, to 3am Fri & Sat; 🚇5A, 6A, 14, 150S, Ⓜ Nørreport, Ⓢ Nørreport) channels a fast-fading Copenhagen. The menu is unapologetically hearty, generous and cheap for this part of town, with faithful *smørrebrød*, *frikadeller* (Danish meatballs) and *pariserbøf* (minced beef steak with egg and onions). The deceptively named *mini-platte* offers a satisfying overview of classic Nordic flavours. Whatever you choose, wash it down with a (very generous) shot of akvavit.

enough to leave you purring. (📞33 14 46 46; www.laglace.dk; Skoubogade 3; cake slices 62kr, pastries 39-49kr; 🕐8.30am-6pm Mon-Fri, 9am-6pm Sat, 10am-6pm Sun; 📶🚻; 🚇14)

Drinking

Ved Stranden 10
WINE BAR

12 🍷 MAP P64, G5

Politicians and well-versed oenophiles make a beeline for this canal-side wine bar and its enviable cellar stocked with classic European vintages, biodynamic wines and more obscure drops. With modernist Danish design and friendly, clued-in staff, its string of

Board Games & Beer

A godsend on rainy days, hugely popular, supercosy **Bastard Café** (📞 42 74 66 42; https://bastardcafe.dk; Rådhusstræde 13; ⏰ noon-midnight Sun-Thu, to 2am Fri & Sat; 🚌 1A, 2A, 9A, 14, 26, 37) is dedicated to board games, which line its rooms like books in a library. Some are free to use, while others incur a small 'rental fee'. While away the hours playing an old favourite or learn the rules of a more obscure option.

rooms lend an intimate, civilised air that's perfect for grown-up conversation. Discuss terroir and tannins over vino-friendly nibbles like olives, cheeses and smoked meats. (📞 35 42 40 40; www.vedstranden10.dk; Ved Stranden 10; ⏰ noon-10pm Mon-Sat; 🛜; 🚌 1A, 2A, 9A, 26, 37, 66, 350S, 🅼 Kongens Nytorv)

Ruby

COCKTAIL BAR

13 🚇 MAP P64, E5

Cocktail connoisseurs raise their glasses to high-achieving Ruby, hidden away in an unmarked 18th-century townhouse. Inside, suave mixologists whip up near-flawless, seasonal libations created with craft spirits and homemade syrups, while a lively crowd spills into a labyrinth of cosy, decadent rooms. For a gentlemen's club

vibe, head downstairs among chesterfields, oil paintings and wooden cabinets lined with spirits. (📞 33 93 12 03; www.rby.dk; Nybro-gade 10; ⏰ 4pm-2am, from 6pm Sun; 🛜; 🚌 1A, 2A, 14, 26, 37, 🅼 Gammel Strand)

Mother Wine

WINE BAR

14 🚇 MAP P64, F2

A *hyggelig* (cosy) wine bar/shop with some very prized Finn Juhl chairs, Mother Wine showcases natural, organic and lesser-known Italian drops. From organic Veneto Prosecco to Puglian Negroamaro, guests are encouraged to sample the day's rotating offerings before committing to a glass. Wines start at a very palatable 55kr and come with a small complimentary serve of Italian nibbles. (📞 33 12 10 00; http://motherwine.dk; Gammel Mønt 33; ⏰ 10am-7pm Mon-Wed, to 10pm Thu & Sat, to late Fri; 🛜; 🚌 350S, 🅼 Kongens Nytorv)

1105

COCKTAIL BAR

15 🚇 MAP P64, G3

Head in before 11pm for a bar seat at this dark, luxe lounge. Named for the local postcode, its cocktail repertoire spans both the classic and the revisited. You'll also find a fine collection of whiskies, not to mention an older 30- and 40-something crowd more interested in thoughtfully crafted drinks than partying hard and getting wasted. (📞 33 93 11 05; www.1105.dk; Kristen Bernikows Gade 4; ⏰ 8pm-2am

Wed, Thu & Sat, 4pm-2am Fri; 🚌1A, 26, 350S, Ⓜ Kongens Nytorv)

Democratic Coffee
COFFEE

16 🟢 MAP P64, D3

Democratic Coffee is not your typical library coffee shop, and it's not just for students: it's popular with locals and tourists alike. The long wooden coffee bar offers espresso as well as V60-brewed coffee, and the freshly baked croissants (20kr) have been called the best in the city, especially the popular almond variety. (Watch your clothes: the filling is rich and runny.) (🖉40 19 62 37; Krystalgade 15; ⏱8am-7pm Mon-Fri, 9am-4pm Sat; 📶; 🚌14, Ⓜ Nørreport, Ⓢ Nørreport)

Entertainment

Jazzhus Montmartre
JAZZ

17 ⭐ MAP P64, G2

Saxing things up since the late 1950s, this is one of Scandinavia's great jazz venues, with past performers including Dexter Gordon, Ben Webster and Kenny Drew. Today, it continues to host local and international talent. On concert nights, you can also tuck into a decent, three-course set menu (325kr) at the **cafe-restaurant** from 6pm. (🖉tickets 70 20 20 96, venue 91 19 19 19; www.jazzhusmontmartre.dk; Store Regnegade 19A; ⏱varies, see website; 🚌1A, 26, Ⓜ Kongens Nytorv)

Jazzhus Montmartre

Danish Design

Visit a Copenhagen home and you'll invariably find Poul Henningsen lamps hanging from the ceiling, Arne Jacobsen or Hans Wegner chairs in the dining room, and the table set with Royal Copenhagen dinner sets, Stelton cutlery and Bodum glassware. Here, good design is not just for museums and institutions: it's an integral part of daily life.

Iconic Chairs

Modern Danish furniture is driven by the principle that design should be tailored to the comfort of the user – a principle most obvious in Denmark's world-famous designer chairs. Among the classics is Hans Wegner's Round Chair (1949). Proclaimed 'the world's most beautiful chair' by US *Interiors* magazine in 1950, it would find fame as the chair used by Nixon and Kennedy in their televised presidential debates in 1960. The creations of modernist architect Arne Jacobsen are no less iconic. Designed for Copenhagen's Radisson Blu Royal Hotel, the Egg Chair (1958) is the essence of jet-setting mid-century modernity. His revolutionary Ant Chair (1952), the model for stacking chairs found in schools and cafeterias worldwide, found infamy as the chair on which call girl Christine Keeler (from the British Profumo Affair) sat in a 1960s Lewis Morley photograph.

Switched-on Lighting

Danish design prevails in stylish lamps as well. The country's best-known lamp designer was Poul Henningsen (1894–1967), who emphasised the need for lighting to be soft, for the shade to cast a pleasant shadow and for the light bulb to be blocked from direct view. His PH5 lamp (1958) remains one of the most popular hanging lamps sold in Denmark today. The popularity of fellow modernist designer Verner Panton is no less enduring. Like Henningsen, Panton was interested in creating lighting that hid the light source, a goal achieved to playful effect with his signature Flowerpot lamp (1968). The designer, who worked for Arne Jacobsen's architectural office from 1950 to 1952, would also go down as an innovative furniture designer, his plastic single-piece Panton Chair (1967) one of the 20th century's most famous furniture pieces.

Shopping

Hay House DESIGN

18 🅰 MAP P64, F4

Rolf Hay's fabulous interior design store sells its own coveted line of furniture, textiles and design objects, as well as those of other fresh, innovative Danish designers. Easy-to-pack gifts include anything from notebooks and ceramic cups, to building blocks for style-savvy kids. (📞42 82 08 20; www.hay.dk; Østergade 61; ⊙10am-6pm Mon-Fri, to 5pm Sat; 🚌1A, 2A, 9A, 14, 26, 37, 66, Ⓜ Kongens Nytorv)

Stilleben DESIGN

19 🅰 MAP P64, E4

Owned by Danish Design School graduates Ditte Reckweg and Jelena Schou Nordentoft, Stilleben stocks a bewitching range of contemporary ceramics, glassware, jewellery and textiles from mostly emerging Danish and foreign designers. Head up the wooden stairs for posters and prints, including works by celebrated contemporary Danish artist Cathrine Raben Davidsen. There's a **second branch** opposite gourmet food market Torvehallerne KBH. (📞33 91 11 31; www.stilleben.dk; Niels Hemmingsensgade 3; ⊙10am-6pm Mon-Fri, to 5pm Sat; 🚌1A, 2A, 9A, 14, 26, 37, 66, Ⓜ Kongens Nytorv)

Cinemateket

Cinephiles flock to the Danish Film Institute's **Cinemateket** (📞33 74 34 12; www.dfi.dk; Gothersgade 55; ⊙9.30am-10pm Tue-Fri, noon-10pm Sat, noon-7.30pm Sun; 🚌350S), which screens around 70 films per month, including twice-monthly classic Danish hits (with English subtitles) on Sundays. The centre also houses an extensive library of film and TV literature, a 'videotheque' with more than 1500 titles – including feature films, shorts, documentaries and TV series – as well as a shop and restaurant-cafe.

Illums Bolighus DESIGN

20 🅰 MAP P64, F4

Design fans hyperventilate over this sprawling department store, its four floors packed with all things Nordic and beautiful. You'll find everything from ceramics, glassware, jewellery and fashion to throws, lamps, furniture and more. It's also a handy spot to pick up some souvenirs, from posters, postcards and notebooks adorned with vintage Danish graphics to design-literate Danish wallets and key rings. (📞33 14 19 41; www.illumsbolighus.dk; Amagertorv 8-10; ⊙10am-7pm Mon-Thu & Sat, to 8pm Fri, 11am-6pm Sun; 🚻; 🚌1A, 2A, 9A, 14, 26, 37, 66, Ⓜ Kongens Nytorv)

Many of Copenhagen's museums are closed on Mondays (especially outside the summer season), making Monday the ideal day for a little Danish retail therapy. The worst day to shop is Sunday, when numerous smaller stores are shut.

Storm   FASHION & ACCESSORIES

21 MAP P64, G2

Storm is one of Copenhagen's most inspired fashion pit stops, with trendsetting men's and women's labels such as Haider Ackermann, Kitsuné and Thom Browne. The vibe is youthful and street smart, with extras including statement trainers, boutique fragrances, art and design tomes, fashion magazines and jewellery. Obligatory for the cashed-up, street-smart style crew. (33 93 00 14; www.stormfashion.dk; Store Regnegade 1; 11am-5.30pm Mon-Thu, to 7pm Fri, 10am-4pm Sat; 1A, 26, 350S, Kongens Nytorv)

NN07   FASHION & ACCESSORIES

22 MAP P64, G3

This is the striking flagship store for Danish menswear brand NN07 (aka: No Nationality). The clothes here are understated and contemporary, ranging from soft jersey tees and street-smart sweat tops, to stylish knits, crisp-collared shirts and chinos in easy-to-match block colours. These goods aren't cheap, but the quality is high and the pieces are designed to last. Accessories include leather belts and bags. (38 41 11 41; www.nn07.com; Gammel Mønt 7; 10am-6pm Mon-Thu, to 7pm Fri, to 5pm Sat, noon-4pm Sun; 1A, 26, 350S, Kongens Nytorv)

Baum und Pferdgarten   FASHION & ACCESSORIES

23 MAP P64, F2

Designers Rikke Baumgarten and Helle Hestehave are the creative forces behind what is one of Denmark's most respected women's fashion brands. While there's no shortage of pared-back Copenhagen chic, the collections here always fuse a sense of quirkiness, fun and subversiveness. Expect sharp, structured silhouettes, playful prints and beautiful fabrics. (35 30 10 90; www.baumund pferdgarten.com; Vognmagergade 2; 10am-6pm Mon-Thu, to 7pm Fri, to 5pm Sat; 350S, Kongens Nytorv)

Posterland   GIFTS & SOUVENIRS

24 MAP P64, G2

Posterland is Northern Europe's biggest poster company and the main art supplier for the gallery shops of the National Gallery of Denmark and the Louisiana Museum of Modern Art. Spruce up your walls with art, travel and vintage posters, as well Copenhagen-themed posters showcasing iconic locations like Tivoli Gardens and the Carlsberg Brewery. (33 11 28 21; www.posterland.dk; Gothersgade 45;

⊙9.30am-6pm Mon-Thu, to 7pm Fri, to 5pm Sat; 🚌350S, 🅼Kongens Nytorv)

⊙11am-6pm Mon-Fri, 10am-5pm Sat; 🚌350S, 🅼Kongens Nytorv)

Han Kjøbenhavn
FASHION & ACCESSORIES

25 🔒 MAP P64, F2

While we love the uncluttered Modernist fit-out, it's what's on the racks that will hook you: simple, beautifully crafted men's clothes that merge Scandinavian sophistication with street smarts and a hint of old-school Danish working-class culture. The label has often collaborated with other designers, like Australian shoemaker Teva and American woolwear veteran Pendleton. In-store accessories include Han's own range of painfully cool eyewear. (www.hankjobenhavn.com; Vognmagergade 7, 52 15 35 07;

Wood Wood
FASHION & ACCESSORIES

26 🔒 MAP P64, G3

Unisex Wood Wood's flagship store is a solid spot for distinctive street fashion. Top of the heap are Wood Wood's own playful creations, made with superlative fabrics and attention to detail. The supporting cast includes trainers, unconventional clothing from designers like Comme des Garçons Play, Peter Jansen and Gosha Rubchinskiy, as well as accessories spanning fragrances and wallets to quirky eyewear. (📞35 35 62 64; www.woodwood.dk; Grønnegade 1; ⊙10.30am-6pm Mon-Thu, to 7pm Fri, to 5pm Sat, noon-4pm Sun; 🚌1A, 26, 350S, 🅼Kongens Nytorv)

Hay House (p73)

YADID LEVY/ALAMY ©

Explore ✦

Nyhavn & the Royal Quarter

The canal of Nyhavn (pronounced 'new-hown') was long a haunt for sailors and writers, including Hans Christian Andersen. These days it lures tourists with its colourful gabled town houses, ship masts and foaming ale. Behind its bustle is blue-blooded Frederiksstaden, home to the royal palace, Marmorkirken (Marble Church) and, further north, the less impressive Little Mermaid.

The Short List

○ **Designmuseum Danmark (p78)** *Get a crash course in design culture and history in a converted rococo hospital.*

○ **Nyhavn (p82)** *Capture Copenhagen's colour-popping historic waterfront, former address of Hans Christian Andersen.*

○ **Amalienborg Slot (p82)** *Snoop around the Danish royals' downtown digs, adorned with nostalgic interiors and storybook guards.*

○ **Rebel (p83)** *Treat yourself to a tasting menu where French and Danish influences conspire to great effect.*

○ **Meyers Bageri (p85)** *Devour luscious baked goods from a pioneer of the New Nordic food movement.*

Getting There & Around

Ⓜ Kongens Nytorv station lies 200m southwest of Nyhavn.

🚌 Take route 1A for the Royal Quarter and Østerbro and route 26 for Statens Museum for Kunst. Catch the 350S for Botanisk Have (Botanic Garden) and Nørrebro. Route 66 runs from Nyhavn to Slotsholmen and onward to Tivoli Gardens and Central Station.

⚓ Harbour buses stop at Nyhavn.

Nyhavn & the Royal Quarter Map on p80

Top Experience 📷

Admire Danish Design at the Designmuseum

Don't know your Egg from your Swan? What about your PH4 from your PH5? For a crash course in Danish design, head for Designmuseum Danmark. Housed in a converted 18th-century hospital, the museum is a must for fans of the applied arts and industrial design, its collection exploring the evolution of one of the world's most emulated design cultures.

◉ MAP P80, D4

📞 33 18 56 56

www.designmuseum.dk

Bredgade 68

adult/child 115kr/free

🕐 10am-6pm Tue & Thu-Sun, to 9pm Wed

🚌 1A, Ⓜ Kongens Nytorv

Twentieth-Century Crafts & Design

This is the museum's hero permanent exhibition, exploring 20th-century industrial design and crafts in the context of social, economic, technological and theoretical changes. You'll find a wealth of Danish design classics, among them Børge Mogensen's Shaker table. One small room dedicated to Arne Jacobsen features objects the architect specifically created for his SAS Royal Hotel. More unusual highlights include Henningsen's steel, timber and leather PH Grand Piano, as well as a wall of vintage graphic posters that includes the work of Viggo Vagnby, creator of the iconic 1959 'Wonderful Copenhagen' poster.

Fashion & Fabric

A notable permanent exhibition is *Fashion & Fabric*, a showcase for the museum's rich cache of textiles, fashion and accessories. Broken down into three main themes – Design and Decoration, Handicrafts and Industry, and Body and Identity – the 500-plus items on display span four centuries of production. And while the booty includes international creations, the focus is on Danish ingenuity, whether it be brocaded rococo silk dresses and corded-quilted gowns, *hedebo* embroidery or millinery.

Temporary Exhibitions

The museum's rotating temporary exhibitions provide fresh insights into the collection and design in general. Recent shows include *Learning from Japan*, an exploration of the role traditional Japanese crafts and applied arts have played in the development of Danish design. Other temporary offerings have included a pop-up exhibition dedicated to Finnish architect Alvar Aalto and his modernist masterpiece, Paimio Sanatorium.

★ Top Tip

○ The museum shop is one of the city's best. You'll find beautiful, design-orientated books, unique ceramics, glassware and jewellery. You'll also find a small selection of Copenhagen-designed fashion pieces.

✕ Take a Break

○ Head to the museum's **Klint Cafe** (☑33 18 56 86; https://design museum.dk/besog-os/ cafe; Designmuseum Danmark, Bredgade 68; smørrebrød 60-85kr; ⏰10am-5.30pm Tue & Thu-Sun, to 8.30pm Wed; 🚌1A) for salads, smørrebrød and sweet treats. In the warmer months, diners can kick back in the museum's historic, leafy courtyard.

○ If it's dinnertime, savour seasonal dishes, cured meats and quality wines at nearby Pluto (p112).

Nyhavn & the Royal Quarter Admire Danish Design at the Designmuseum

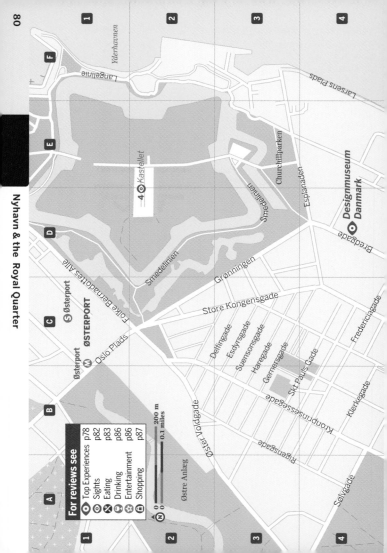

Yderhavnen

Langelinie

Larsens Plads

Kastellet

4

Churchillparken

Smedelinien

Designmuseum
Danmark

Esplanaden

Bredgade

Smedelinien

Grønningen

Smedelinien

Østerport

ØSTERPORT

Folke Bernadottes Allé

Store Kongensgade

Oslo Plads

Østerport

DELINIEN

Delfingade

Esdyrsgade

Suensonsgade

Haregade

Gernersgade

Skt Pauls Gade

Fredericiagade

Kronprinsessegade

Klerkegade

Øster Voldgade

Rigensgade

Sølvgade

Østre Anlæg

For reviews see

◉	Top Experiences	p78
◎ ◉	Sights	p82
✕	Eating	p83
🍸	Drinking	p86
🎭	Entertainment	p86
🛍	Shopping	p87

0   200 m
0   0.1 miles

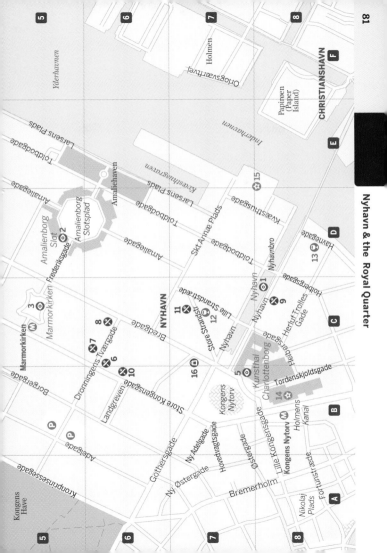

5

6

7

8

F CHRISTIANSHAVN

E

D

C

B

A

Yderhavnen

Holmen

Orlogsværftvej

Papirøen
(Paper
Island)

Inderhavnen

Toldbodgade

Larsens Plads

Amaliegade

Kvæsthusgraven

Larsens Plads

15

Kvæsthusgade

Amalienborg
Slot

2

Amalienborg
Slotsplad

Amaliehaven

Toldbodgade

Skt Annæ Plads

Nyhavnbro

Nyhavn

Holbergsgade

13

Havnegade

Amaliekirken

Marmorkirken

Frederiksgade

Amaliegade

Toldbodgade

Lille Strandstræde

Nyhavn

1

Nyhavn

9

Herluf Trolles
Gade

M 3

Marmorkirken

Borgergade

8

NYHAVN

11

Store Strandstræde

12

Nyhavn

Kunsthal
Charlottenborg

Heibergsgade

Bredgade

Dronningens Tværgade

7

6

10

Landgreven

Store Kongensgade

16

Kongens
Nytorv

5

Holmens
Kanal

14

Tordenskjoldsgade

Kongens
Have

Borgergade

Adelgade

P

P

Kronprinsessegade

Gothersgade

Ny Adelgade

Hovedvagtsgade

Østergade

M Kongens Nytorv

Lille Kongensgade

Bremerholm

Ny Østergade

Fortunstræde

Nikolaj
Plads

5

6

7

8

Sights

Nyhavn

CANAL

1 ◎ MAP P80, C8

There are few nicer places to be on a sunny day than sitting at an outdoor table at a cafe on the quayside of the Nyhavn canal. The canal was built to connect Kongens Nytorv to the harbour and was long a haunt for sailors and writers, including Hans Christian Andersen. He wrote *The Tinderbox, Little Claus and Big Claus* and *The Princess and the Pea* while living at No 20, and also spent time living at Nos 18 and 67. (Nyhavn; 🚌 1A, 26, 66, 350S, Ⓜ Kongens Nytorv)

Amalienborg Slot

PALACE

2 ◎ MAP P80, D5

Home of the current queen, Margrethe II, Amalienborg Slot consists of four austere 18th-century palaces around a large cobbled square. The changing of the guard takes place here daily at noon, the new guard having marched through the city centre from the barracks on Gothersgade at 11.30am. (☎ 33 15 32 86; www.kongernessamling.dk/amalienborg; Amalienborg Plads; adult/child 95kr/free; ⊙ 10am-5pm daily mid-Jun–mid-Sep, reduced hours rest of year; 🚌 1A, 26)

Amalienborg Slot

NIKOLPETR/SHUTTERSTOCK ©

Marmorkirken CHURCH

3 ◉ MAP P80, C5

Consecrated in 1894, the neo-baroque Marble Church (officially Frederikskirken) is one of Copenhagen's most imposing architectural assets. Its grandiose dome – inspired by St Peter's in Rome and the largest church dome in Scandinavia – offers an impressive view over the city. The church was ordered by Frederik V and drawn up by Nicolai Eigtved. Construction began in 1749 but spiralling costs saw the project mothballed. Salvation came in the form of Denmark's wealthiest 19th-century financier CF Tietgen, who bankrolled the project's revival. (Marble Church; 📞 33 15 01 44; www.marmorkirken.dk; Frederiksgade 4; dome adult/child 35/20kr, church admission free; ⏱church 10am-5pm Mon-Thu & Sat, from noon Fri & Sun, dome 1pm daily mid-Jun–Aug, 1pm Sat & Sun rest of year; 🚌1A)

Kastellet FORTRESS

4 ◉ MAP P80, D2

The star-shaped fortress of Kastellet was originally commissioned by Frederik III in 1662. Today, it is one of the most historically evocative sites in the city, its grassy ramparts and moat surrounding some beautiful 18th-century barracks, as well as a chapel occasionally used for concerts. On the ramparts is a historic windmill, and you get some excellent views of the harbour and Marmorkirken's Vatican-like dome. (🚌1A, 🚏Nordre Toldbod)

Kunsthal Charlottenborg MUSEUM

5 ◉ MAP P80, B7

Fronting Kongens Nytorv, Charlottenborg was built in 1683 as a palace for the royal family. Home to Det Kongelige Kunstakademi (Royal Academy of Fine Arts) since 1754, it is also a spacious venue for topical contemporary art from homegrown and international names. Expect anything from site-specific installations and video art to painting and sculpture. Admittedly, shows here can be a little hit or miss, so check what's on before heading in. (📞33 74 46 39; www.kunsthalcharlottenborg.dk; Nyhavn 2; adult/child 75kr/free, after 5pm Wed free; ⏱noon-8pm Tue-Fri, 11am-5pm Sat & Sun; 🚌1A, 26, 350S, Ⓜ Kongens Nytorv)

Eating

Rebel DANISH $$$

6 🍴 MAP P80, C6

Smart, split-level Rebel dishes out arresting, modern Danish grub without the fanfare. The dining space is relatively unadorned, giving all the attention to inspired creations like braised octopus with crispy chicken, sage and mushroom foam. Trust the sommelier's wine choices, which include extraordinary Old and New World drops. (📞33 32 32 09; www.restaurantrebel.dk; Store Kongensgade 52; menu incl. wine 875kr, small dishes 95-270kr; ⏱5.30pm-midnight Tue-Sat; 🚌1A, 26, Ⓜ Kongens Nytorv)

District Tonkin VIETNAMESE $

7 🍴 MAP P80, C6

With a playful interior channelling the streets of Vietnam, casual, convivial District Tonkin peddles fresh, gut-filling *bánh mì* (Vietnamese baguettes), stuffed with coriander, fresh chilli and combos like Vietnamese sausage with marinated pork, homemade pâté and BBQ sauce. The menu also includes gorgeous, less-common Vietnamese soups, among them tomato-based *xíu mai* (with pork and mushroom meatballs). (📞60 88 86 98; http://district-tonkin.com; Dronningens Tværgade 12; baguettes 58-62kr, soups & salads 70-120kr; ⏱11am-9.30pm Sun-Wed, to 10pm Thu-Sat; 🚌1A, 26, Ⓜ️Kongens Nytorv)

AOC NEW NORDIC $$$

8 🍴 MAP P80, C6

In the vaulted cellar of a 17th-century mansion, this intimate, two-starred Michelin standout thrills with evocative, often surprising Nordic flavour combinations, scents and textures. Here, sea scallops might conspire with fermented asparagus, while grilled cherries share the plate with smoked marrow and pigeon breast. Diners choose from two tasting menus, and reservations should be made around a week in advance, especially for late-week dining. (📞33 11 11 45; www.restaurantaoc.dk; Dronningens Tværgade 2; tasting menu 2000kr; ⏱6.30-9:30pm Tue-Sat; 📶; 🚌1A, 26, Ⓜ️Kongens Nytorv)

Cinnamon and raisin swirl

Gorm's

PIZZA $$

9 MAP P80, C8

Right on Nyhavn canal, rustic, wood-beamed Gorm's is one of the city's best pizza joints. The bases here are thin, crispy and made with sourdough. Toppings are high quality, with both Italian imports and local artisanal items (Funen lamb salami, anyone?). Libations include a handful of local craft beers and a longer cast of cocktails, among them a liquorice-spiked espresso martini. (☑60 40 12 02; www.gormspizza.dk; Nyhavn 14; pizzas 120-145kr; ☺noon-10.30pm Sun-Thu, to 11.30pm Fri & Sat; 🚌66, 🚇Kongens Nytorv)

Meyers Bageri

BAKERY $

10 MAP P80, B6

Sugar and spice and all things nice is what you get at this pocket-sized organic bakery, owned by the founding father of the New Nordic food movement, Claus Meyer. Only Danish flour ground in-house is good enough for these sticky morsels, among them golden apple croissants, *blåbærsnurrer* (blueberry twists) and a luscious *kanelsnægel* (cinnamon snail) laced with *remonce* (creamed butter and sugar filling). (www.clausmeyer.dk; Store Kongensgade 46; pastries from 14kr; ☺7am-6pm Mon-Fri, to 4pm Sat & Sun; 🚌1A, 26, 🚇Kongens Nytorv)

Mystery Makers

Bring out your inner Detective Sarah Lund with a **Mystery Makers** (☑30 80 30 50; http://mysterymakers.dk; Mystery Hunt per person 250-300kr, Escape Room per person 250-400kr; ☺hours vary; 🚌1A, 🚇Østerport) interactive mystery hunt. Offered at numerous historical sites around town, players are given fictional identities and a mystery to solve, with a series of riddles and clues along the way. Suitable for adults and kids aged 12 and above, you will need a minimum of four people to form a team. See the website for pricing, which varies according to the day of the week and time of day. (Sunday to Wednesday before 3pm is cheapest.)

Union Kitchen

CAFE $$

11 MAP P80, C7

Around the corner from touristy Nyhavn is cognoscenti Union Kitchen, where inked staffers look like punk-pop rockers, the palette is grey on grey, and the clipboard menu is packed with quality, brunch-friendly grub, from yoghurt and granola to burgers and seasonal salads. Top choices include waffles and the 'Balls of the Day',

Forloren Espresso

Coffee snobs weep joyfully into their nuanced espressos and Third-Wave brews at snug, light-filled Forloren Espresso. Bespectacled owner Niels tends to his brewing paraphernalia like an obsessed scientist, turning UK- and Swedish-roasted beans into smooth, lingering cups of Joe. If you're lucky, you'll score the cosy back nook, the perfect spot to browse Niels' collection of photography tomes.

the latter a combo of succulent homemade meatballs served with interesting sides. (Store Strandstræde 21; dishes 79-159kr; ⏱7.30am-midnight Mon-Fri, from 8am Sat, 8am-5pm Sun; 🛜; 🚌1A, 66, Ⓜ Kongens Nytorv)

Drinking

Nebbiolo   WINE BAR

12 🚇 MAP P80, C7

Just off Nyhavn, this smart, contemporary wine bar and shop showcases wines from smaller, inspiring Italian vineyards. Wines by the glass are priced in one of three categories (75/100/125kr) and even those in the lowest price range are often wonderful. (📞60 10 11 09; http://nebbiolo-winebar. com; Store Strandstræde 18; ⏱3pm-midnight Sun-Thu, to 2am Fri & Sat; 🛜; 🚌1A, 66, Ⓜ Kongens Nytorv)

Den Vandrette   WINE BAR

13 🚇 MAP P80, D8

This is the harbourside wine bar for lauded wine wholesaler **Rosforth & Rosforth** (📞33 32 55 20; www.rosforth.dk; Knippelsbrogade 10; ⏱9am-5pm Mon-Fri, from noon Sat; 🚌2A, 9A, 37, 350S, Ⓜ Christianshavn). The focus is on natural and biodynamic drops, its short, sharply curated list of wines by the glass often including lesser-known blends like Terret Bourret–Vermentino. Guests are welcome to browse the cellar and pick their own bottle. Come summer, it has alfresco waterside tables and deckchairs for sun-kissed toasting. (📞72 14 82 28; www.denvandrette.dk; Havnegade 53A; ⏱4-11pm Mon-Sat; 🚌66, 🚢Nyhavn)

Entertainment

Det Kongelige Teater   BALLET, OPERA

14 ⭐ MAP P80, B8

These days, the main focus of the opulent Gamle Scene (Old Stage) is world-class opera and ballet, including productions from the Royal Danish Ballet. The current building, the fourth theatre to occupy the site, was completed in 1872 and designed by Vilhelm Dahlerup and Ove Petersen. Book tickets in advance. (Royal Theatre; 📞33 69 69 69; https://kglteater. dk; Kongens Nytorv; 🚌1A, 26, 350S, Ⓜ Kongens Nytorv)

Skuespilhuset   THEATRE

15 ⭐ MAP P80, E8

Copenhagen's harbourside playhouse is home to the Royal Danish Theatre and a world-class repertoire of homegrown and foreign plays. Productions range from the classics to provocative contemporary works. Tickets often sell out well in advance, so book ahead if you're set on a particular production. English-language tours (120kr) are available in July and August; see the website for details. (Royal Danish Playhouse; 📞33 69 69 69; https://kglteater.dk; Sankt Anne Plads 36; 🚌66, ⛴Nyhavn, Ⓜ Kongens Nytorv)

Shopping

Klassik Moderne Møbelkunst   DESIGN

16 🔒 MAP P80, C7

Close to Kongens Nytorv, Klassik Moderne Møbelkunst is Valhalla for lovers of Danish design, with a trove of classics from greats like Poul Henningsen, Hans J Wegner, Arne Jacobsen, Finn Juhl and Nanna Ditzel – in other words, a veritable museum of Scandinavian furniture from the mid-20th century. (📞33 33 90 60; www.klassik. dk; Bredgade 3; 🕑11am-6pm Mon-Fri, 10am-4pm Sat; 🚌1A, 26, 350S, Ⓜ Kongens Nytorv)

Skuespilhuset

Explore
Christianshavn

Christianshavn channels Amsterdam with its snug canals, outdoor cafes and alternative attitude. The quarter was established by Christian IV in the early 17th century as a commercial centre and also as a military buffer for the expanding city. Equally reminiscent of hyper-liberal Amsterdam is the area's most famous attraction, the hash-scented, live-and-let-live commune of Christiania.

The Short List

◦ **Christiania (p90)** *Let your hair down in Copenhagen's alt-living heartland, where bucolic paths lead to eclectic abodes.*

◦ **Vor Frelsers Kirke (p95)** *Scale a sky-high spiral tower inspired by Italian architect Francesco Borromini.*

◦ **Kadeau (p96)** *Secure a table at a two-starred Michelin powerhouse.*

◦ **Christianshavns Bådudlejning & Café (p99)** *Watch the world float by at a much-loved canalside café.*

◦ **Operæn (p99)** *Give in to a night of intrigue, passion and pathos at Copenhagen's spectacular, harbourfront Opera House.*

Getting There & Around

Ⓜ Christianshavn station is on Torvegade, Christianshavn's main thoroughfare.

🚌 Routes 2A, 40 and 350 cross Christianshavn along Torvegade. Take routes 2A and 37 for Tivoli Gardens and Central Station; route 350S for Nørrebro; and bus 9A for Christiania and Operaen.

🚢 Harbour buses stop at Operæn. Alternatively, disembark at Nyhavn and cross the Inderhavnsbroen pedestrian bridge to Christianshavn.

Christianshavn Map on p94

Christianshavn DIEGO GRANDI/SHUTTERSTOCK ©

Top Experience 📷
Wander Free-Spirited Christiania

Picturesque Christiania is more about its canals, historic streets and leafy ramparts than must-see sights. One exception is world-famous commune Christiania, the city's stubbornly idealistic '1970s child'. The commune is within easy walking distance of Christianshavn metro station and its canal-side location makes it a beautiful spot for a quiet water-side saunter. The historic, architecturally unique Vor Freslers Kirke and Christians Kirke are also within easy walking distance of the metro station.

👁 MAP P94, D3

www.christiania.org

Prinsessegade

🚌 9A, Ⓜ Christianshavn

Dyssen

Dyssen is Christiania's best-kept secret. This long, pencil-thin rampart on the eastern side of the old city moat is connected to Christiania's eastern edge by bridge. Running north–south along the rampart is a 2km-long path, studded with beautiful maples and ash, hawthorn, elder and wild cherry trees, not to mention the homes of some rather fortunate Christianites. It's a perfect spot for lazy ambling, slow bike rides or some quiet downtime by the water among the swans, herons, moorhens and coots. Some locals even head here to forage for edible snails. Yet Dyssen has a dark past. The rampart was the site of Denmark's last execution ground, where 29 convicted Nazi sympathisers faced the firing squad following the country's postwar trials. The final execution, taking place in 1950, was of Niels Rasmus Ib Birkedal Hansen, the most senior Danish member of the Gestapo. Eerily, the concrete floor and drain are still visible by the path at the northern end of Dyssen.

Stadens Museum for Kunst

Christianites refer to Christiania as 'Staden' (The Town), and the name of art gallery Stadens Museum for Kunst is a tongue-in-cheek play on the more 'establishment' Statens Museum for Kunst. You'll find the place on the 2nd floor of the Loppen building, a former artillery warehouse dating from 1863 and flanking Prinsessegade, just beside Christiania's main entrance. Head up for rotating exhibitions of contemporary art, spanning both local and international artists, and covering anything from drawings and paintings to installations. In any given month you might be poring over Greenlandic stoneware, recycled Tunisian sculpture or local photography. The gallery also houses a petite cafe for any caffeine-fuelled art debate you may be itching to have.

★ Top Tips

○ From late June to the end of August, 60- to 90-minute guided tours (40kr) of Christiania run daily at 3pm (weekends only September to late June). Tours commence just inside Christiania's main entrance on Prinsessegade.

○ While taking photos in Christiania is generally fine, don't snap pictures on or around the main drag of Pusher St. The area is lined with illegal cannabis dealers who can become nervous or aggressive if photographed.

✕ Take a Break

For affordable vegetarian grub in a pretty garden, make a beeline for Morgenstedet (p97), located in the heart of Christiania.

For a more upmarket dinner, reserve a table at Michelin-starred, modern-Danish hotspot 108 (p97), located 650m north of Christiania.

Den Grå Hal

The Grey Hall is the commune's largest cultural venue, able to pack in around 1500 people. It was built in 1893, originally as a riding hall for the military. With the establishment of Freetown Christiania, the space found new purpose as a hub for art and music. Some of the biggest names in music have rocked its weathered walls over the years, among them Bob Dylan, Metallica and Manic Street Preachers. While its calendar is hardly jam-packed these days, the building is worth a look for its architecture and colourful graffiti. In December Den Grå Hal becomes the focal point for Christiania's Christmas festivities, which include a Yuletide market.

DIY Architecture

Beyond its graffiti-strewn barrack buildings, Christiania is home to some of the city's most eclectic, imaginative architecture. Much of this is in the form of 'tiny houses', small abodes built by hand using salvaged materials. Follow the commune's quieter paths and you'll stumble upon a whimsical collection of buildings, from a home made entirely of random window frames to converted greenhouses, German *bauwagens* (wooden caravans) and Roma wagons, and houses on boats and floating platforms. Many of the most intriguing creations are located beside, or close to, the old city moat on Christiania's eastern side. Needless to say, these are private abodes, so remember to be respectful and considerate.

Loppen

Its motto might be 'Going out of business since 1973', but 40-something **Loppen** (📞 32 57 84

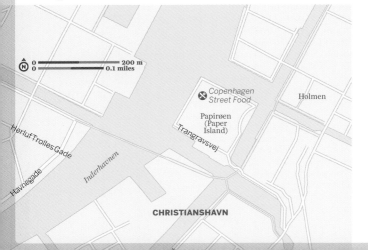

Stadens Museum for Kunst (p91)

22; www.loppen.dk; Sydområdet 4B; 8.30pm-late Sun-Thu, 9pm-late Fri & Sat; ; 9A, 2A, 37, 350S, Christianshavn) just keeps on rocking. In the same wooden-beamed warehouse as art gallery Stadens Museum for Kunst, the joint started off by spotlighting the local underground scene before evolving into a more prolific music hub. These days, its program serves up an eclectic mix of both local and international talent, from emerging acts to more established names. Indeed, past guests have included top-tier acts like Smashing Pumpkins and Animal Collective.

Christianshavn

0   200 m
0   0.2 miles

Holmen

Retshalevej

Fabriksområdet

Kløvermærket

F

Ekvipagemesterevej

⭐ 10

Inderhavnen

Papirøen (Paper Island)

Halvtolv

Holmen

Stadsgraven

E

Christianshavn

Pusher St

⊙ Christiania

Vor Frelsers Kirke

✗ 5
✗ 6

Overgaden Neden Vandet

CHRISTIANSHAVN

Prinsessegade

Overgaden Oven Vandet

Sofiegade

Christianshavn

⓪ 10

D

NYHAVN

Skt Annæ Plads

Nyhavn

Bredgade

Herluf Trolles Gade

Havnegade

✗ 8

Strandgade

M Christianshavn

Dronningensgade

🍷 9

⊙ 2

Overgaden Oven Vandet

✗ 4

Christians Kirke

⊙ 3

Wildersgade

Torvegade

C

Gothersgade

Kongens Nytorv

M Kongens Nytorv

Tordenskjoldsgade

Holmens Kanal

Bremerholm

Christian IV's Bro

Slotsholms Kanal

Knippelsbro

Børsgade

Cirkelbroen Bridge

Inderhavnen

B

Gammel Mønt

Pilestræde

Gammel Strand

M Gammel Strand

Vindebrogade

Holmens Bro

Christiansborg Slot

Christiansborg

Ministerialbygning

SLOTSHOLMEN

Christians Brygge

Langebro

A

1
2
3
4

N

Sights

Vor Frelsers Kirke
CHURCH

1 MAP P94, C4

It's hard to miss this 17th-century church and its 95m-high spiral tower. For a soul-stirring city view, make the head-spinning 400-step ascent to the top – the last 150 steps run along the outside rim of the tower, narrowing to the point where they literally disappear at the top. Inspired by Borromini's tower of St Ivo in Rome, the spire was added in 1752 by Lauritz de Thurah. Inside the church, highlights include an ornate baroque altar and elaborately carved pipe organ from 1698. (📞 41 66 63 57; www.vorfrelserskirke.dk; Sankt Annæ Gade 29; church free, tower adult/ child 40/10kr; 🕙 11am-3.30pm, closed during services, tower 9.30am-7pm Mon-Sat, 10.30am-7pm Sun May-Sep, reduced hours rest of year; 🚌 2A, 9A, 37, 350S, Ⓜ Christianshavn)

Overgaden
GALLERY

2 MAP P94, C4

Rarely visited by tourists, this non-profit art gallery runs about 10 exhibitions annually, putting the spotlight on contemporary installation art and photography, usually by younger artists, both Danish and international. The gallery also runs a busy calendar of artist talks, lectures, performances, concerts and film screenings. See the website for upcoming events. (📞 32 57 72 73; www.overgaden.org; Overgaden Neden Vandet 17; admission free;

Vor Frelsers Kirke

⏱1-5pm Tue, Wed & Fri-Sun, to 8pm Thu; 🚌2A, 9A, 37, 350S, Ⓜ Christianshavn)

Christians Kirke
CHURCH

3 👁 MAP P94, B4

Named in honour of Christian IV – who founded Christianshavn in the early 17th century – Christians Kirke is well known for its unusual rococo interior. This includes tiered viewing galleries more reminiscent of a theatre than a place of worship. The church was built between 1754 and 1759, serving Christianshavn's sizeable German congregation until the end of the 19th century. (📞32 54 15 76; www.christianskirke.dk; Strandgade 1; ⏱10am-4pm Tue-Fri; 🚌2A, 9A, 37, 350S, Ⓜ Christianshavn)

Eating

Kadeau
NEW NORDIC $$$

4 🍴 MAP P94, C4

The big-city spin-off of the Bornholm original, this Michelin-two-starred standout has firmly established itself as one of Scandinavia's gastronomic powerhouses. Whether it's salted and burnt scallops drizzled with clam bouillon, or an unexpected combination of lardo, thyme, cherry blossom and Korean pine, each dish manages to evoke moods and landscapes with extraordinary creativity and skill.

The wine list is a thrilling, enlightening showcase of smaller producers and natural drops, and service is warm, genuine and knowledgeable. Book ahead. (📞33

Cafe Wilder (p99)

25 22 23; www.kadeau.dk; Wildersgade 10B; tasting menu 2150kr, wine/juice pairings 1350/800kr; ⏱6.30pm-midnight Tue-Sat, also noon-4pm Sat; 🚌2A, 9A, 37, 350S, Ⓜ Christianshavn)

108

DANISH $$

5 🍴 MAP P94, D2

In a soaring, concrete-pillared warehouse, 108 offers a more casual, accessible take on New Nordic cuisine than its world-renowned sibling Noma. The family-style sharing-plate menu is all about seasonal, locally sourced ingredients, farmed or foraged, preserved, fermented and pickled. While not all dishes hit the mark, many leave a lasting impression. Three dishes per diner should satiate most appetites. (📞32 96 32 92; www.108.dk; Strandgade 108; dishes 95-185kr, sharing dishes for 2 people 300-450kr; ⏱restaurant 5pm-midnight, cafe 8am-midnight Mon-Fri, from 9am Sat & Sun; 📶; 🚌9A)

Barr

SCANDINAVIAN $$$

6 🍴 MAP P94, D2

Meaning 'barley' in old Norse, oak-lined Barr offers polished, produce-driven takes on old North Sea traditions. The small plates are a little hit and miss, with standouts including sourdough pancakes with caviar. You'll need about four small plates per person; a better-value option is to savour the pancakes and fill up on the fantastic schnitzel or *frikadeller* (Danish meatballs). (📞32 96 32 93; http://restaurantbarr. com; Strandgade 93; small dishes 75-

Explore in a GoBoat

The **GoBoat** (📞40 26 10 25; www.goboat.dk; Islands Brygge 10; boat hire 1/2/3hr 449/799/1049kr; ⏱9.30am-sunset; 🚼; 🚌5C, 12, Ⓜ Islands Brygge) kiosk beside Islands Brygge Havnebadet rents out small solar-powered boats that let you explore Copenhagen's harbour and canals independently. You don't need prior sailing experience and each comes with a built-in picnic table (you can buy supplies at GoBoat or bring your own). Boats seat up to eight and rates are per boat, so the more in your group, the cheaper per person.

240kr, 4-course menu 600kr; ⏱5pm-midnight Tue-Thu, from noon Sat & Sat; 📶; 🚌9A, 66, 🛥Nyhavn)

Morgenstedet

VEGETARIAN $

7 🍴 MAP P94, E4

A homey, hippy bolthole in the heart of Christiania, Morgenstedet offers a short, simple blackboard menu. There's usually one soup, plus two or three mains with a choice of side salads. Whether it's cauliflower soup with chickpeas and herbs or creamy potato gratin, options are always vegetarian, organic and delicious, not to mention best devoured in the blissful cafe garden. Cash only. (Fabriksområdet 134, Christiania; dishes 50-110kr; ⏱noon-9pm Tue-Sun; 📶🛒; 🚌9A, Ⓜ Christianshavn)

The Danish Table

Not only is Copenhagen home to 15 Michelin stars, it's also the stomping ground of an ever-expanding league of bold, brilliant young chefs turning top produce into groundbreaking innovations and putting new verve into long-loved classics. So grab a (beautifully designed) fork and find a spot at the coveted Danish table.

Beyond New Nordic

While the New Nordic cuisine served at hotspot restaurants like Michelin-starred Kadeau continues to thrill food critics, bloggers and general gluttons, Copenhagen's food scene continues to evolve. Numerous chefs from high-end kitchens have since opened their own restaurants, among them 108, Restaurant Mes and Bror. Most of these offer simpler, more affordable food but don't skimp on quality and innovation: a 'democratisation' of the gourmet dining experience. Many are also taking a less dogmatic approach to contemporary Nordic cooking, using the odd non-regional influence or spice without fear of Nordic culinary damnation. A Noma alumnus is behind hugely popular taquería Hija de Sanchez, one of a growing number of casual, high-quality international eateries that also includes Slurp Ramen Joint.

Danish Classics

Despite the New Nordic revolution, old-school Danish fare remains a major player on the city's tables. Indeed, tucking into classics such as *frikadeller* (meatballs), *sild* (pickled herring) and Denmark's most famous culinary export, smørrebrød (open sandwiches), at institutions such as Schønnemann is an integral part of the Copenhagen experience. The basic smørrebrød is a slice of bread topped with any number of ingredients, from roast beef or pork to juicy shrimps, pickled herring, liver pâté or fried fish fillet. The garnishes are equally variable,with the sculptured final product often looking too good to eat. In the laws of Danish smørrebrød, smoked salmon is served on white bread, and herring on rye bread. Whatever the combination, the iconic dish is best paired with akvavit and an invigorating beer.

Cafe Wilder

DANISH $$

8 MAP P94, C3

With its crisp white linen and circular sidewalk tables, this corner classic feels like a Parisian neighbourhood bistro. It's actually one of Copenhagen's oldest cafes, featured several times in the cult TV series *Borgen*. Relive your favourite scenes over beautiful lunchtime smørrebrød (open sandwiches) or Franco-Danish dinner mains like tender Danish pork with sweet-potato croquette and a blackcurrant sauce. (✆32 54 71 83; www.cafewilder.dk; Wildersgade 56; lunch 119-149kr, dinner mains 179-209kr; ⊙9am-11pm Mon-Thu, to midnight Fri & Sat, to 10.30pm Sun; 🛜; 🚌2A, 9A, 37, 350S, Ⓜ️Christianshavn)

Drinking

Christianshavns Bådudlejning & Café

BAR

9 MAP P94, C4

Right on Christianshavn's main canal, this festive, wood-decked cafe-bar is a wonderful spot for drinks by the water. It's a cosy, affable hang-out, with jovial crowds and strung lights. There's grub for the peckish and gas heaters and tarpaulins to ward off any northern chill. (✆32 96 53 53; www.baadudlejningen.dk; Overgaden Neden Vandet 29; ⊙10am-midnight Jun-Aug, reduced hours rest of year; 🛜; 🚌2A, 9A, 37, 350S, Ⓜ️Christianshavn)

Islands Brygge Havnebadet

Come summer, sun-seeking locals gravitate to **Islands Brygge Havnebadet** (✆30 89 04 69; https://svoemkbh.kk.dk/indhold/havnebade; Islands Brygge; admission free; ⊙24hr Jun-Sep, lifeguards on duty 11am-7pm; 👶; 🚌5C, 12, Ⓜ️Islands Brygge), central Copenhagen's most popular outdoor baths. Located just south of Christianshavn in Islands Brygge, its trio of pools sit right in Copenhagen's inner harbour. Water quality is rigorously monitored and the lawns, BBQ facilities and eateries make it a top spot to see and be seen on a warm summer day, whether you get wet or not.

Entertainment

Operæn

OPERA

10 MAP P94, E1

Designed by the late Henning Larsen, Copenhagen's state-of-the-art opera house has two stages: the Main Stage and the smaller, more experimental Takkeløftet. The repertoire runs the gamut from blockbuster classics to contemporary opera. While the occasional opera is sung in English, all supertitles are in Danish only. Tickets can be booked directly via the website. (Copenhagen Opera House; ✆box office 33 69 69 69; www.kglteater.dk; Ekvipagemestervej 10; 🚌9A, ⛴️Operaen)

Explore ◈

Nørreport

Nørreport and its surrounds blend market stalls, restaurants and bars with distinguished art collections. You'll find appetite-piquing Torvehallerne KBH and the quietly hip strip of Nansensgade dotted with atmospheric eating and drinking spots. The area is also home to several flagship sights, among them Statens Museum for Kunst and Rosenborg Slot. The latter skirts manicured Kongens Have.

The Short List

◦ **Rosenborg Slot (p102)** *Lust after the Danish crown jewels at a Renaissance castle fit for a fairy tale.*

◦ **Statens Museum for Kunst (p106)** *Rub proverbial shoulders with homegrown and international masters at Denmark's progressive national art museum.*

◦ **Torvehallerne KBH (p108)** *Graze, swill and stock the larder with artisanal edibles at Copenhagen's gourmet food market.*

◦ **Davids Samling (p111)** *Envy an exquisite collection of fine and applied art in the former home of a formidable collector.*

◦ **Høst (p111)** *Dine like a top-end epicurean at digestible, kronor-conscious prices.*

Getting There & Around

Ⓜ Nørreport station is right beside Torvehallerne KBH.

🚆 All S-train lines stop at Nørreport station. Catch a Helsingør-bound regional train to Humlebæk for Louisiana Museum of Modern Art.

🚌 Take routes 5C and 350S for Nørrebro. Bus 14 runs through central Copenhagen and is handy for Slotsholmen. Route 6A runs to Vesterbo and Frederiksberg.

Nørreport Map on p110

Rosenborg Slot (p102) SINA ETTMER PHOTOGRAPHY/SHUTTERSTOCK ©

Top Experience 📷
Visit Christian IV's Renaissance Castle

*Moated **Rosenborg Slot** heaves with blue-blooded portraits and tapestries, royal hand-me-downs and the nation's crown jewels. Built between 1606 and 1633 by Christian IV to serve as his summer home, the Danish royals opened the castle as a museum in the 1830s, while still using it as as their own giant jewellery box. It serves both functions to this day.*

◉ MAP P110, D3

📞 33 15 32 86

www.kongernessamling.
dk/en/rosenborg

Øster Voldgade 4A

adult/child 110kr/free

🕘 9am-6pm mid-Jun–
mid-Sep, reduced hours
rest of year

Christian IV's Winter Room

Room 1 is the original building's best-preserved room. The rich wooden panelling – adorned with inlaid Dutch paintings – was begun by Court cabinetmaker Gregor Greuss and completed in 1620. Adorning the ceiling are mythological paintings by Danish-born Dutch painter Pieter Isaacsz, the works replacing the room's original stucco ceiling c 1770. Among the room's items is a 17th-century Florentine tabletop, made of inlaid semi-precious stones. Equally fascinating is the Astronomical Clock, which comes with moving figures and musical works. Dating back to 1594, the timepiece was made by the renowned Swiss clockmaker Isaac Habrecht.

Christian IV's Bedroom

It's in room 3 that Denmark's famous 'Builder King', Christian IV, died on 28 February 1648, and it's here that you'll find his nightcap and slippers, as well as the bloodstained clothes from his naval battle of Kolberger Heide in July 1644. The walls, doors and stucco ceiling all date back to Christian IV's time, as does the stucco ceiling in the adjoining toilet. The toilet's fetching blue and white wall tiles date to Frederik IV's refurbishment of the castle in 1705. Some of the tiles are the Dutch original, while others were made in Copenhagen in 1736. Back in the day, a water cistern was used for flushing, with the king's business expelled straight into the moat.

Mirror Cabinet

It mightn't be the 1st floor's most lavish room, but the Mirror Cabinet is certainly its most curious. Inspired by France's Palace of Versailles, the room's mirrored ceiling, floor and walls could sit comfortably on the pages of a 1970s interior design magazine. In reality, the interior is pure baroque, dating back to the beginning of the 18th century and specially designed for Frederik IV. All the rage at the time, mirror

★ Top Tips

o To avoid the queues – which can be dishearteningly long in the peak summer months – buy your ticket online. The ticket can be sent directly to your smartphone so there's no need to print a copy. Also, buying your ticket online ensures you entry in your desired time slot. If you have a Copenhagen Card, however, you will need to obtain your tickets in person at the castle ticket office.

✕ Take a Break

o On the other side of Kongens Have, **Big Apple** (http://big-apple.dk; Kronprinsessegade 2; sandwiches 60kr; ⏱8am-6pm Mon-Fri, 9am-6pm Sat & Sun; 🛜; 🚌350S, Ⓜ Kongens Nytorv) is a good spot to grab a freshly made sandwich and coffee to enjoy in the park.

cabinets were commonly featured in the innermost sanctum of a king's suite, usually in connection with the royal bedchamber. Frederik IV's bedchamber was downstairs in room 4, connected to the Mirror Cabinet by a spiral staircase. If the thought of all these mirrors seems a little kinky, bear in mind that the adjoining room is where the king kept his collection of erotica.

Knights' Hall

Originally a ballroom, the Knights' Hall was completed in 1624 and was the last of the castle's rooms to be furnished. Gracing the walls are the Rosenborg Tapestries, 12 woven works depicting the battles between Denmark and Sweden during the Scanian War (1675–79). The tapestries were a PR exercise of sorts, commissioned by Christian V to flaunt his military prowess. The Knights' Hall is also home to the coronation thrones and a stucco ceiling with four paintings by Hendrick Krock that represent the four regalia: crown, orb, sword and sceptre. Two small chambers run off the hall, one displaying Venetian glassware, the other home to Royal Copenhagen Porcelain's original Flora Danica set, decorated with exquisite botanical motifs.

Basement Cellar Rooms & Green Room

Rosenborg Slot's undisputed pièce de résistance is its basement, home to an extraordinary collection of royal regalia and gifts. Some of the dusty bottles in the castle cellar date back to the 18th century. The wine is still used on special royal occasions, though it's now merely splashed

Interior of Rosenborg Slot

into more palatable drops as a ceremonial gesture. The northernmost cellar room contains some rather unusual decorative objects, including an 18th-century chandelier made of amber by Lorenz Spengler. At the southern end of the basement is the Green Room, itself laden with intriguing royal paraphernalia. Keep an eye out for Christian IV's riding trappings, used at his coronation in 1596.

Treasury
Just off the Green Room, the Treasury is where you'll find the castle's most valuable treasures. These include Christian IV's spectacular crown, created especially for his coronation by Dirich Fyring in Odense. Made of gold, pearls and table-cut stones and weighing 2.89kg, its features include the figure of a self-pecking pelican feeding its offspring blood (a symbolic representation of the need for rulers to willingly sacrifice their own blood for their subjects.) Other showstoppers include the jewel-studded sword of Christian III (crafted in 1551) and the obsessively detailed Oldenburg Horn. Made of silver in the mid-15th century, the horn is believed to have been a gift from Christian I to Cologne's cathedral. It found itself in Danish hands once more after the Reformation.

Kongens Have
Fronting Rosenborg Slot is much-loved Kongens Have (King's Garden). The city's oldest park, it was laid out in the early 17th century by Christian IV, who used it as his vegetable patch. These days it has a little more to offer, including wonderfully romantic paths, a fragrant rose garden and some of the longest mixed borders in northern Europe. It's also home to a marionette theatre, with free performances from mid-July to mid-August (2pm and 3pm Tuesday to Sunday). Located on the northeastern side of the park, the theatre occupies one of the neoclassical pavilions designed by 18th-century Danish architect Peter Meyn.

Top Experience 📷

Explore Denmark's Top-Tier Art Museum

Denmark's **Statens Museum for Kunst** *(National Gallery) is the country's pre-eminent art institution, its cache of paintings, sculpture and immersive works spanning centuries of creative expression, from Mategna to Matisse and beyond. Top billing goes to its homegrown heavyweights: Golden Age icons, such as Christoffer Wilhelm Eckersberg and Christen Købke.*

◉ MAP P110, D1

📞 33 74 84 94

www.smk.dk

Sølvgade 48-50

adult/child 120kr/free

🕐 11am-5pm Tue & Thu-Sun, to 8pm Wed

🚌 6A, 26, 42, 184, 185

European Art: 1300–1800

Originally a royal collection, this is where you'll find the museum's Old Masters. These include Rubens' blockbuster *Judgement of Solomon* (c1617; pictured). Look out for a series of paintings by 17th-century Flemish artist Cornelis Norbertus Gijsbrechts: trompe l'œils with an astoundingly modern sensibility. Standout Italian works include Andrea Mategna's *Christ as the Suffering Redeemer* (c1495–1500).

Danish & Nordic Art: 1750–1900

Don't miss the quiet rage of Nicolai Abildgaard's *Wounded Philoctetes* (1775) and Johan Christian Dahl's *Winter Landscape near Vordingborg, Denmark* (1829). CW Eckersberg's most celebrated work is *A View through Three Arches of the Third Storey of the Colosseum* (1815–16). What appears to be a faithful panorama of Rome is actually pieced together from three different perspectives.

French Art: 1900–30

SMK's French collection includes an impressive number of works by Henri Matisse. The most famous of these is *Portrait of Madame Matisse* (1905). Also known as *The Green Line*, it's widely considered a masterpiece of modern portrait painting. Other standouts here include André Derain's *Woman in a Chemise* (1906) – a highlight from the artist's Fauvist period.

Modern Danish & International Art

The collection's modern Danish works are especially notable, among them expressionist Jens Søndergaard's brooding *Stormy Sea* (1954) and CoBrA artists such as Asger Jorn. Look out for Bjørn Nørgaard's *The Horse Sacrifice* and *Objects from the Horse Sacrifice*, which document the artist's ritualistic sacrifice of a horse in 1970 to protest the Vietnam War.

★ Top Tips

○ Consider exploring the collections with SMK's fantastic audio guide. Selected highlights for the permanent collections are discussed in short, easily digestible interviews with a museum curator.

○ The museum hosts numerous special events throughout the year. These include SMK Fridays. Held around seven times annually (in spring and autumn), it sees the museum open until late with art talks, DJs, performances and food. Check the website for details.

✕ Take a Break

○ Just 450m east of the National Gallery, **Aamanns Takeaway** (☎20 80 52 01; www.aamanns.dk; Øster Farimagsgade 10; smørrebrød 65-115kr; ⏰11am-5.30pm daily, take away 11am-7pm Mon-Fri, to 4pm Sat & Sun; 🚌6A, 14, 37, 42, 150S, 184, 185) serves some of the best smørrebrød in the city.

Walking Tour 🥾

Spend a Day in Norreport

A mouthwatering ode to the fresh, the tasty and the slow, food market **Torvehallerne KBH** (www.torvehallernekbh.dk; Israels Plads; dishes from around 55kr; ⏰10am-7pm, to 10pm Fri, to 6pm Sat, 11am-5pm Sun; Ⓜ Nørreport, Ⓢ Nørreport) *peddles everything from seasonal herbs and berries, to smoked meats, seafood and cheeses, smørrebrød, fresh pasta, and hand-brewed coffee. You could easily spend an hour or more exploring its twin glass halls, chatting to the vendors, stocking the larder, and noshing on freshly cooked, sit-down meals.*

Walk Facts
Start Grød

Finish Noorbohandelen

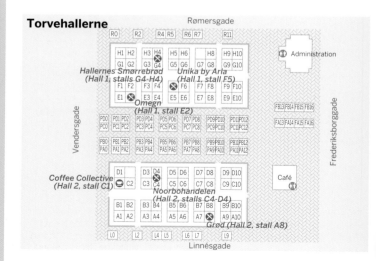

❶ Grød

Holistic **Grød** (📞50 59 82 15;
http://groed.com; Stall A8, Hall 2,
Torvehallerne KBH; breakfast 45-75kr,
lunch 65-85kr; ⏰7.30am-7pm Mon-Fri,
9am-6pm Sat & Sun; 📶; 🚌5E, 150S,
185, Ⓜ Nørreport, Ⓢ Nørreport) turns
stodge sexy with its modern take
on porridge. Made-from-scratch
options might include porridge
with gooseberry compote, liquo-
rice sugar, *skyr* (Icelandic yogurt)
and hazelnuts. If it's later in the
day, try the chicken congee.

❷ Coffee Collective

Save your caffeine fix for **Coffee
Collective** (www.coffeecollective.
dk; Stall C1, Hall 2, Torvehallerne KBH;
⏰7am-8pm Mon-Fri, 8am-7pm Sat,
8am-6pm Sun). The beans here
are sourced ethically and directly
from farmers and the team usually
offers two espresso blends: one
full-bodied and traditional, the
other more stringent and Third
Wave in flavour.

❸ Omegn

Nordic deli **Omegn** (Stall E2, Hall
1, Torvehallerne KBH; cheese & charcuterie platter 70-95kr; ⏰10am-7pm
Mon-Thu, to 8pm Fri, to 6pm Sat, 11am-
5pm Sun; 📶; Ⓜ Nørreport, Ⓢ Nørreport, Ⓢ 15E, 150S, 185) stocks the top
products from various small-scale
Danish farms and food artisans.
The cheese selection includes
Thybo, a sharp cow's milk cheese
from northern Jutland. Another
good buy are the handcrafted
Borghgedal beers from Vejle.

❹ Unika

Arla is one of Denmark's mega
dairy companies, and **Unika by
Arla** (📞76 43 44 39; www.arlaunika.
dk; Stall F5, Hall 1, Torvehallerne KBH;
⏰10am-7pm Mon-Thu, to 8pm Fri, to
6pm Sat, 11am-5pm Sun; 🚌15E, 150S,
185, Ⓜ Nørreport, Ⓢ Nørreport) is its
boutique offshoot. The company
works with small dairies, artisan
cheesemakers and top chefs to
produce Nordic-inspired cheeses.
Look out for the unpasteurised Kry,
which delivers a flavour considered
superior to pasteurised cheeses.

❺ Hallernes Smørrebrød

Not only is the smørrebrød
scrumptious at **Hallernes Smørrebrød** (📞60 70 47 80; www.hallernes.
dk; Stall F2, Hall 1, Torvehallerne KBH;
smørrebrød 52-98kr; ⏰10am-7pm Mon-
Thu, to 8pm Fri, to 6pm Sat, 11am-5pm
Sun; 📶; 🚌15E, 150S, 185, Ⓜ Nørreport, Ⓢ Nørreport), it – like the beers
and snaps on offer – is well priced.
Grab a spot at the wooden bar,
order a Mikkeller beer, and tuck into
beautifully presented classics like
fiskefilet (fish fillet) with remoulade.

❻ Noorbohandelen

It's never too early for a skål at
Noorbohandelen (Hall 2, stall
C4-D4) its shelves stocked with
limited-edition and small-batch
craft spirits to sample and purchase. Options include their own
brand of snaps and bitters, infused
with herbs from the Danish island
of Møn.

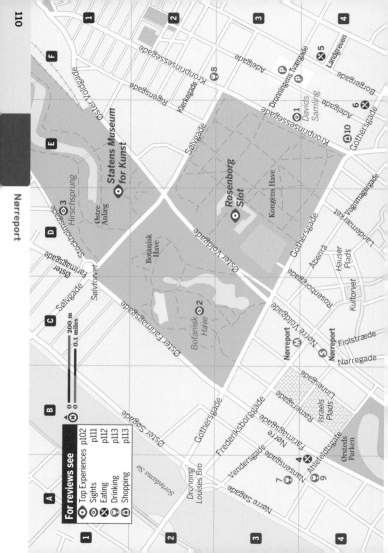

Nørreport

For reviews see
◉ Top Experiences p102
◎ Sights p111
✕ Eating p112
🍸 Drinking p113
🛍 Shopping p113

200 m
0.1 miles

Østervoldgade

Øster Farimagsgade

Stockholmsgade

Sølvgade

Solvtorvet

Hirschsprung 3

Østre Anlæg

Statens Museum for Kunst ◉

Botanisk Have

Botanisk Have 2

Øster Voldgade

Øster Søgade

Sortedams Sø

Dronning Louises Bro

Gothersgade

Frederiksborggade

Nansensgade

Vendersgade

Nørre Farimagsgade

Ahlefeldtsgade

Ørsteds Parken

Israels Plads

Linnésgade

Rømersgade

Nørregade

Fiolstræde

Nørreport Ⓜ

Nørreport Ⓢ

Nørre Voldgade

Rosenborggade

Landemærket

Hauser Plads

Åbenrå

Kultorvet

St Vognmagergade

Gothersgade

Kongens Have

Rosenborg Slot ◉

Kronprinsessegade

Sølvgade

Klerkegade

Øster Voldgade

Rigensgade

Kronprinsessegade

Adelgade

Dronningens Tværgade

Davids Samling ◎1

Adelgade

Borgergade

Gothersgade

8 ◎

5 ✕ Landgreven

6 ✕

10 🛍

7

4

9

Sights

Davids Samling   MUSEUM

1 ⊙ MAP P110, E3

Davids Samling is a wonderful curiosity of a gallery housing Scandinavia's largest collections of Islamic art, including jewellery, ceramics and silk, and exquisite works such as an Egyptian rock crystal jug from AD 1000 and a 500-year-old Indian dagger inlaid with rubies. And it doesn't end there, with an elegant selection of Danish, Dutch, English and French art, porcelain, silverware and furniture from the 17th to 19th centuries. (☑ 33 73 49 49; www.davidmus.dk; Kronprinsessegade 30; admission free; ☺ 10am-5pm Tue & Thu-Sun, to 9pm Wed; 🚌 26, 350S, Ⓜ Kongens Nytorv)

Botanisk Have   GARDENS

2 ⊙ MAP P110, C2

Restorative and romantic, Copenhagen's Botanic Garden lays claim to around 13,000 species of plant life – the largest collection in Denmark. You can amble along tranquil trails, escape to warmer climes in the 19th-century **Palmehus** (☺ 10am-5pm daily Apr-Sep, 10am-3pm Tue-Sun Oct-Apr) glasshouse and even pick up honey made using the garden's own bees at the gorgeous little gift shop. (Botanic Garden; http://botanik.snm.ku.dk; Gothersgade 140, Nørreport; ☺ 8.30am-6pm Apr-Sep, to 4pm Tue-Sun Oct-Mar; 🚹; 🚌 6A, 42, 150S, 184, 185, Ⓜ Nørreport, Ⓢ Nørreport)

Hirschsprung   MUSEUM

3 ⊙ MAP P110, D1

Dedicated to Danish art of the 19th and early 20th centuries, Hirschsprungske is a little jewel-box of a gallery, full of wonderful surprises for art lovers unfamiliar with the classic era of Danish oil painting. Originally the private holdings of tobacco magnate Heinrich Hirschsprung, it contains works by Golden Age painters such as Christen Købke and CW Eckersberg, a notable selection by Skagen painters PS Krøyer and Anna and Michael Ancher, and also works by the Danish symbolists and the Funen painters. (☑ 35 42 03 36; www.hirschsprung.dk; Stockholmsgade 20; adult/child 75kr/free; ☺ 11am-4pm Wed-Sun; 🚌 6A, 14, 37, 42, 150S)

Eating

Høst   NEW NORDIC $$$

4 🍴 MAP P110, A4

Høst's phenomenal popularity is easy to understand: award-winning interiors and New Nordic food that's equally fabulous and filling. The set menu is superb, with smaller 'surprise dishes' thrown in and evocative creations like birch-smoked scallops with horseradish and green beans, or a joyful blueberry sorbet paired with Norwegian brown cheese and crispy caramel. (☑ 89 93 84 09; https://cofoco.dk/en/restaurants/hoest; Nørre Farimagsgade 41; 3-/5-course menu 350/450kr; ☺ 5.30pm-midnight,

KIEV.VICTOR/SHUTTERSTOCK ©

Botanisk Have (p111)

last orders 9.30pm; Ⓜ Nørreport, Ⓢ Nørreport)

Pluto

DANISH $$

5 ❌ MAP P110, F4

Loud, convivial Pluto is not short of friends, and for good reason: superfun soundtrack, attentive staff and beautiful, simple dishes by respected local chef Rasmus Oubæk. Whether it's flawlessly seared cod with seasonal carrots or a side of new potatoes, funky truffles and green beans in a mussel broth, the family-style menu is all about letting the produce sing. (☏33 16 00 16; http://restaurantpluto.dk/forside; Borgergade 16; mains 135-225kr; ⏱5.30pm-midnight Mon-Thu, to 2am Fri & Sat, to 11pm Sun; 🛜; 🚌1A, 26, Ⓜ Kongens Nytorv)

Atelier September

CAFE $

6 ❌ MAP P110, E4

It might look like a *Vogue* photo shoot with its white-on-white interior and vintage glass ceiling (typical of old Danish pharmacies), but Atelier September is very much a cafe. Kitted out in vintage exhibition posters and communal tables, it sells gorgeous espresso and simple, inspired edibles. Standouts include sliced avocado on rye bread, topped with lemon zest, chives, paprika and peppery olive oil. (☏26 29 57 53; www.atelierseptember.dk; Gothersgade 30; dishes 30-125kr; ⏱7.30am-4pm Mon-Fri, from 9am Sat, from 10am Sun; 🚌350S, Ⓜ Kongens Nytorv)

Drinking

Bibendum
WINE BAR

7 🔵 MAP P110, A3

In a snug, rustic cellar on Nansensgade, Bibendum is an oenophile's best friend. While the savvy wine list offers over 30 wines by the glass, always ask the barstaff what's off the menu. On our last visit, this included a spectacular Pinot Noir from the Czech Republic. The vibe is intimate but relaxed and the menu of small plates (80kr to 95kr) simply gorgeous. (📞33 33 07 74; http://bibendum.dk; Nansensgade 45; ⏰4pm-midnight Mon-Sat; 📶; 🚌37, 5C, 350S, Ⓜ️Nørreport, Ⓢ Nørreport)

Culture Box
CLUB

8 🔵 MAP P110, F2

Electronica connoisseurs swarm to Culture Box, known for its impressive local and international DJ line-ups and sharp sessions of electro, techno, house and drum'n'bass. The club is divided into three spaces: pre-clubbing Culture Box Bar, intimate club space Red Box, and heavyweight Black Box, where big-name DJs play the massive sound system. (📞33 32 50 50; www.culture-box.com; Kronprinsessegade 54A; ⏰Culture Box Bar 6pm-1am Thu-Sat, Red Box 11pm-late Fri & Sat, Black Box midnight-late Fri & Sat; 🚌26)

Bankeråt
BAR

9 🔵 MAP P110, A4

A snug spot to get stuffed (literally), kooky, attitude-free Bankeråt is decorated with taxidermic animals in outlandish get-ups – yes, there's even a ram in period costume. The man behind it all is local artist Filip V Jensen. But is it art? Debate this, and the mouth-shaped urinals, over a local craft beer (a much better choice than the very average wines). If you're feeling hungry, Bankeråt offers customised burgers (149kr). Best of all, part of the bar's profits go to helping sponsor kids. (📞33 93 69 88; www.bankeraat.dk; Ahlefeldtsgade 27; ⏰9.30am-11pm Mon & Tue, to midnight Wed-Fri, 10.30am-midnight Sat, 10.30am-8pm Sun; 📶; 🚌37, 5C, 350S, Ⓜ️Nørrebro, Ⓢ Nørrebro)

Shopping

Stine Goya
FASHION & ACCESSORIES

10 🔒 MAP P110, E4

The winner of numerous prestigious design awards, Stine Goya is one of Denmark's hottest names in women's fashion. What makes her collections unique is the ability to marry clean Nordic simplicity with quirky details. Not cheap but highly collectable. (📞32 17 10 00; www.stinegoya.com; Gothersgade 58; ⏰11am-6pm Mon-Fri, to 4pm Sat; 🚌350S, Ⓜ️Kongens Nytorv)

Explore ◈

Nørrebro

Gritty Nørrebro subverts the Nordic stereotype with its dense, sexy funk of art-clad 19th-century tenements, multicultural crowds and thronging cafes and bars. Despite being home to Assistens Kirkegård – the final resting place of Hans Christian Andersen – this corner of the city is less about sights and more about independent stores and galleries, craft beers and kaleidoscopic street life.

The Short List

◦ **Assistens Kirkegård (p119)** *Amble or picnic among late Danish legends in an enchanting old cemetery.*

◦ **Oysters & Grill (p119)** *Slurp fresh seafood and boozy cocktails at a loud, convivial stalwart.*

◦ **Coffee Collective (p122)** *Sip a sustainable single origin brew on one of the city's coolest neighbourhood strips.*

◦ **Bæst (p119)** *Tuck into home-made charcuterie, cheese and wood-fired pizza perfection at Christian Puglisi's bustling local bistro.*

◦ **Brus (p121)** *Taste-test out-of-the-box craft beers and kegged cocktails from rock-star indie brewer To Øl.*

Getting There & Around

🚌 Routes 5C and 350S connect the city centre to Nørrebro. Both routes run along Nørrebrogade, Nørrebro's main thoroughfare.

Nørrebro Map on p118

Walking Tour 🥾

Nørrebro Soul

Nørrebro is Copenhagen's creative heart, a multiethnic enclave splashed with quirky parks and street art, intriguing workshops and studios, as well as the city's most beautiful eternal resting place. So tie up those trainers and hit the pavement for red squares and bulls, giant birds and tankers, and a shady street turned good.

Start Superkilen; bus 5A to Nørrebrogade

End Jægersborggade; bus 8A to Jagtvej

Length 2km; 1.5 hours

❶ Superkilen

Created by local architecture studio Bjarke Ingels Group, Berlin-based landscape architects Topotek1 and Danish art group Superflex, the 1km-long park **Superkilen** is a hyper playful ode to the area's multicultural fabric, with Russian neon signs, Ghanaian bollards, and even a Spanish bull.

❷ Basco5 Mural

Head east along Mimersgade, turning left into Bragesgade. On the side of number 35 is a **street art mural** by Copenhagen artist Nils Blishen, better known as Basco5. Birds, bearded men and a round, cartoonish style are all trademarks of the artist's work.

❸ BaNanna Park

Turn right into Nannasgade and walk 250m to oil refinery turned playground **BaNanna Park**. Its striking gateway is a 14-metre-high climbing wall, popular with active locals and open to all (BYO climbing equipment).

❹ Odinsgade Murals

Two blocks ahead is Odinsgade. The whimsical mural on the side of number 17 is by Simon Hjermind Jensen, Anne Sofie Madsen and Claus Frederiksen. The adjacent tanker mural uses existing architectural features to dramatic effect.

❺ Assistens Kirkegård

At Jagvej, turn right, and continue to hallowed **Assistens Kirkegård** (p119). In 2013 the cemetery created a 75-sq-metre burial plot for the city's homeless, complete with a bronze sculpture by artist Leif Sylvester. Each day, eccentric local Captain Irishman collects flowers for the plot.

❻ Jægersborggade

Directly opposite Assistens Kirkegård, Jægersborggade is a vibrant hub of craft studios, boutiques and eateries. At no 45, **Vanishing Point** (p123) showcases quirky local ceramics, jewellery, handmade knits, quilts and engaging, limited-edition prints, much of it made on site. At No 48, **Gågron!** (p123) peddles design-literate everyday products with a conscience.

✕ Take a Break
End your saunter with superlative coffee at **Coffee Collective** (p122).

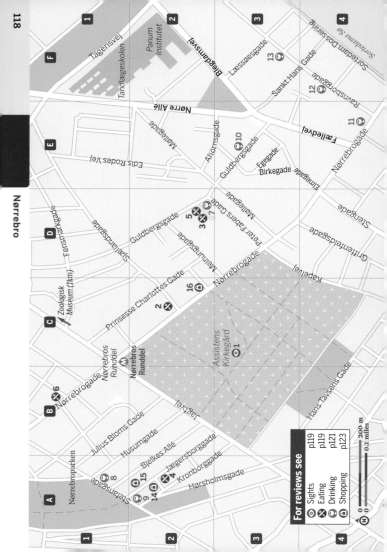

1 F

Tagensvej

Tandlægeskolen

Panum Institutet

2

Blegdamsvej

3

Sortedam Dossering

Læssøesgade

13

Sankt Hans Gade

12

Ravnsborggade

4

Nørre Allé

Møllegade

E

Edis Rodes Vej

Ahornsgade

Guldbergsgade

10

Eggegade

Elmegade

Birkegade

11

Fælledvej

Nørrebrogade

Fensmarksgade

Sjællandsgade

D

Guldbergsgade

Meinungsgade

Peter Fabers Gade

Møllegade

5

3

7

Stengade

Griffenfeldsgade

Zoologisk
Museum (1km)

Prinsesse Charlottes Gade

Rantzausgade

16

Nørrebrogade

Nørrebrogade

Kapelvej

2

C

Norrebros
Runddel

M Nørrebros
Runddel

Assistens
Kirkegård

1

B

Nørrebrogade

6

Nørrebrogade

Jagtvej

Hans Tavsens Gade

Julius Bloms Gade

Husumgade

Bjelkes Allé

Jægersborggade

Kronborggade

Hørsholmsgade

A

Nørrebroparken

Stefansgade

8

15

9

14

4

For reviews see

⊙	Sights	p119
⊗	Eating	p119
⊙	Drinking	p121
⊞	Shopping	p123

200 m
0.1 miles

1

2

3

4

Sights

Assistens Kirkegård   CEMETERY

1 👁 MAP P118, C3

You'll find some of Denmark's most celebrated citizens at this famous cemetery, including philosopher Søren Kierkegaard, physicist Niels Bohr, author Hans Christian Andersen and artists Jens Juel, Christen Købke and CW Eckersberg. It's a wonderfully atmospheric place to wander around – as much a park and garden as it is a graveyard. A good place to start is at the main entrance on Kapelvej, where you can usually find fold-out maps of the cemetery and its notable burial sites. (📞35 37 19 17; http://assistens.dk; Kapelvej 4, Nørrebro; ⏰7am-10pm Apr-Sep, to 7pm Oct-Mar; 🚌5C, 8A)

Eating

Oysters & Grill   SEAFOOD $$

2 🍴 MAP P118, C2

Finger-licking surf and turf is what you get at this rocking, unpretentious neighbourhood favourite, complete with kitsch vinyl tablecloths and a fun, casual vibe. The shellfish is fantastically fresh and, unlike most places, ordered by weight, which means you don't need to pick at measly servings. Meat lovers won't to be disappointed either, with cuts that are lustfully succulent. (📞70 20 61 71; www.cofoco.dk/da/restauranter/oysters-and-grill; Sjællandsgade 1B, Nørrebro; mains 165-245kr; ⏰5.30pm-midnight daily; 🚌5C)

Cemetery Picnic

It might sound macabre, but historic cemetery Assistens Kirkegård is a popular picnic and sunbathing spot in the warmer months. Graced with leafy, tranquil nooks, it's a blissful spot to spend a lazy afternoon reading a good book or simply contemplating the beauty of life...and maybe cheese.

Bæst   ITALIAN $$

3 🍴 MAP P118, D2

Owned by powerhouse Italo-Scandi chef Christian Puglisi, Bæst remains hot. Charcuterie, cheese and competent woodfired pizzas are the drawcards here. Much of the produce is organic, and both the commendable charcuterie and hand-stretched mozzarella are made upstairs (the latter made using jersey milk from Bæst's own farm). To fully appreciate its repertoire, opt for the sharing menu (small/large 375/450kr). (📞35 35 04 63; www.baest.dk; Guldbergsgade 29, Nørrebrø; pizzas 85-145kr; ⏰5-10.30pm, plus noon-3pm Thu-Sun; 🛜; 🚌3A, 5C)

Relæ   NEW NORDIC $$$

4 🍴 MAP P118, A2

Established by prolific chef Christian Puglisi, Relæ was one of the first restaurants in town to offer superlative New Nordic cooking

Eco Capital

While some Western governments continue to debate the veracity of climate-change science, Denmark gets on with innovative, sustainable business. Indeed, the Danish capital is well on its way to becoming the world's first carbon neutral capital by 2025.

Green Mobility

Implementation of the CPH 2025 Climate Plan's focus areas – energy consumption, energy production, green mobility and city-administration initiatives – is visible across the city. As part of the plan, hundreds of city buses have been upgraded with special air filters that cut pollution by 95%.

Denmark's capital is crisscrossed by over 400km of safe, connected bike paths, and even the traffic lights are programmed to give cyclists precedence in peak hour. Less than 30% of local households own a car and, for the first time in 2016, the number of bikes trumped the number of cars in the city centre.

Ditching the Dirt

Ready to remind Copenhageners of the pressing nature of environmental matters is the city's new waste-to-energy plant, Amager Bakke. Designed by local architecture firm Bjarke Ingels Group (BIG), the world's cleanest incineration plant includes a chimney that blows out smoke rings (made of ecofriendly water vapour) for each 250kg of carbon dioxide released into the atmosphere. It's a novel reminder of the importance of reducing carbon emissions.

For Copenhagen, this also involves a hand from its harbour. City energy utility company HOFOR uses an innovative district cooling system that utilises local seawater to provide cooling services to businesses in central Copenhagen. The system saves around 70% of the energy used by traditional air-conditioning systems. Copenhagen harbour itself is an environmental success story: the once heavily polluted waterway is now clean enough for swimming.

without all the designer fanfare. One Michelin star later, it remains a low-fuss place, where diners set their own table, pour their own wine and swoon over soul-lifting dishes focused on seasonality, simplicity and (mostly) organic produce. Book ahead. (📞 36 96 66 09; www.restaurant-relae.dk; Jægersborggade 41, Nørrebrø; 4-/7-course menu 475/895kr; ⏰ 5-10pm Tue-Sat, also noon-1.30pm Fri & Sat; 🚌 8A, 5C)

Mirabelle

CAFE $

5 ✕ MAP P118, D2

Decked out with bold geometric floor tiles, artisan bakery-cafe Mirabelle is owned by Michelin-lauded chef Christian Puglisi, who also owns popular restaurant Bæst next door. It's a slick, contemporary spot for made-from-scratch pastries, simple breakfast bites like eggs Benedict, and a short menu of Italo-centric lunch and dinner dishes, including home-made charcuterie, cheeses and organic-flour pasta. Good coffee to boot. (☑ 35 35 47 24; http://mirabelle-bakery.dk; Guldbergsgade 29, Nørrebro; pastries from 28kr, sandwiches 65kr, lunch & dinner dishes 115-175kr; ☺ 7am-10pm; ☎; ⌨3A, 5C)

Møller

BREAKFAST $

6 ✕ MAP P118, B1

Møller is a cosy and rustic all-day-breakfast haven with a focus on quality local ingredients. Eggs, meats, cheeses, breads and more are offered individually so you can create your own meal according to your tastes – a sort of tapas-style breakfast. The home-made sourdough bread, fresh nuggets with mayo, and the half avocado filled with crumbed almonds, chilli and crème fraiche are especially delicious. (☑ 31 50 51 00; www.kaffeogkoekken.dk; Nørrebrogade 160, Nørrebrø; breakfast dishes 18-46kr; ☺ 9am-4pm; ☎; ⌨5C)

Drinking

Brus

MICROBREWERY

7 🍺 MAP P118, D2

What was once a locomotive factory is now a huge, sleek, hip brewpub. The world-renowned microbrewery behind it is To Øl, and the bar's 30-plus taps offer a rotating selection of To Øl standards and small-batch specials, as well as eight on-tap cocktails. The barstaff are affable and happy to let you sample different options before you commit. (☑ 75 22 22 00; http://tapperietbrus.dk; Guldbergsgade 29F, Nørrebro; ☺ 3pm-midnight Mon-Thu, noon-3am Fri & Sat, noon-midnight Sun; ☎; ⌨5C)

Mikkeller & Friends

MICROBREWERY

8 🍺 MAP P118, A1

Looking suitably cool with its turquoise floors and pale ribbed wood, Mikkeller & Friends is a joint venture of the Mikkeller and To Øl breweries. Beer geeks go gaga over the 40 artisan draft beers and circa 200 bottled varieties, which might include a chipotle porter or an imperial stout aged in tequila barrels. Limited snacks include dried gourmet sausage and cheese. (☑ 35 83 10 20; www.mikkeller.dk/location/mikkeller-friends; Stefansgade 35, Nørrebro; ☺ 2pm-midnight Sun-Wed, to 2am Thu & Fri, noon-2am Sat; ☎; ⌨5C, 8A)

Coffee Collective

COFFEE

9 MAP P118, A2

Copenhagen's most prolific microroastery, Coffee Collective has helped revolutionise the city's coffee culture. Head in for rich, complex cups of caffeinated magic. The baristas are passionate about their single-origin beans and the venue itself sits at one end of creative Jægersborggade in Nørrebro. There are several other outlets, including at gourmet food market Torvehallerne KBH (p108) and in Frederiksberg (p138). (www.coffeecollective.dk; Jægersborggade 57, Nørrebro; ⏰7am-7pm, from 8am Sat & Sun; 🚌8A, Ⓜ Nørrebros Runddel)

Rust

CLUB

10 MAP P118, E3

A smashing, multilevel place attracting one of the largest, coolest, most relaxed crowds in Copenhagen. Live acts focus on alternative or upcoming indie rock, hip-hop or electronica. At 11pm, the venue transforms into a club, with local and international DJs pumping out anything from classic hip-hop to electro, house and more. (📞35 24 52 00; www.rust.dk; Guldbergsgade 8, Nørrebro; ⏰hours vary; 🛜; 🚌3A, 5C, 350S)

Kassen

BAR

11 MAP P118, E4

Loud, sticky Kassen sends livers packing with its dirt-cheap drinks and happy-hour specials (80kr cocktails, anyone?). Guzzle unlimited drinks on Wednesdays for 250kr, with two-for-one deals running the rest of the week: all night Thursdays, 4pm to 10pm Fridays and 8pm to 10pm Saturday. (📞42 57 22 00; http://kassen.dk; Nørrebrogade 18B, Nørrebro; ⏰8pm-late Wed, Thu & Sat, from 4pm Fri; 🚌5C)

Kind of Blue

BAR

12 MAP P118, F4

Chandeliers, heady perfume and walls painted a hypnotic 1950s blue: the spirit of the Deep South runs deep at intimate Kind of Blue. Named after the Miles Davis album, it's never short of a late-night hipster crowd, kicking back porters and drinking in owner Claus' personal collection of soul-stirring jazz, blues and folk. (📞26 35 10 56; www.kindofblue.dk; Ravnsborggade 17, Nørrebro; ⏰4pm-midnight Mon-Wed, to 2am Thu-Sat; 🛜; 🚌5A, 350S)

Nørrebro Bryghus

BREWERY

13 MAP P118, F3

This now-classic brewery kickstarted the microbrewing craze more than a decade ago. While its in-house restaurant serves a decent lunchtime burger as well as fancier New Nordic dishes in the evening, head here for the beers, including the brewery's organic draught beer and a string of fantastic bottled options, from pale and brown ales to 'The Evil', a malty, subtly smokey imperial porter. (📞35 30 05 30; www.noerrebrobryghus.dk; Ryesgade 3, Nørrebro; ⏰noon-11pm Mon-Thu, to 1am Fri & Sat, to 10pm Sun; 🚌3A, 5C, 350S)

Shopping

Vanishing Point · HANDICRAFTS

14 🔒 MAP P118, A2

On trendy Jægersborggade, Vanishing Point is a contemporary craft shop and studio showcasing quirky ceramics, unique jewellery, handmade knits and quilts, as well as engaging, limited-edition prints. Most items are created on-site, while some are the result of a collaboration with non-profits around the world. The aim: to inspire a sustainable and playful lifestyle through nature, traditional craft techniques and humour. (📞25 13 47 55; www.vanishing-point.dk; Jægersborggade 45, Nørrebro; 🕙11am-5.30pm Mon-Fri, to 6pm Sat, to 3pm Sun; 🚌8A)

Gågrøn! · HOMEWARES

15 🔒 MAP P118, A2

Gågrøn! peddles design-literate products with a conscience. The focus is on natural fibers and sustainable, recycled and upcycled materials, transformed into simple, stylish products for everyday use. Stock up on everything from kooky animal-shaped cutting boards and stylish cedar-wood serving trays to aprons and toiletry bags made with organic cotton. (📞42 45 07 72; www.gagron.dk; Jægersborggade 48, Nørrebro; 🕙11am-5.30pm Mon-Fri, 10am-3.30pm Sat, 11am-3pm Sun; 🚌8A)

Nørrebro Loppemarked · MARKET

16 🔒 MAP P118, C2

Running alongside the wall of Assistens Kirkegård on Nørrebrogade, this is Denmark's longest flea market, with over 300 metres of stalls. Head in early and rummage for quirky antiques and jewellery, old LPs and art, not to mention the odd Royal Copenhagen porcelain piece. It runs every Saturday from early April to the end of October. (www.berling-samlerting.dk/32693948; Nørrebrogade, Nørrebro; 🕙8am-3pm Sat Apr-Oct; 🚌5C, 8A, 350S)

Vilhelm Dahlerup & Dronning Louises Bro

It is said that no single architect has contributed to Copenhagen's current look as much as Vilhelm Dahlerup (1836–1907). The city's leading architect of the late 19th century, Dahlerup borrowed from a broad spectrum of European Renaissance influences. His Historicist style of architecture shines especially bright in Ny Carlsberg Glyptotek and the glorious Det Kongelige Teater, two exceptional works in a long list of buildings that also include the Hotel d'Angleterre, Pantomime Theatre at Tivoli Gardens, Carlsberg Brewery and Statens Museum for Kunst. The influence of the French Empire Style is palpable in Dahlerup's **Dronning Louises Bro** (🚌5C, Ⓜ Nørreport, Ⓢ Nørreport), the bridge connecting central Copenhagen to Nørrebro.

Walking Tour 🥾

Østerbro

Detractors might call it 'white bread' and boring, but salubrious Østerbro serves up some satisfying urban surprises, including heritage-listed architecture and iconic lakes. The neighbourhood's name means 'East Gate', a reference to the city's old eastern entrance. These days, it's an area best known for its resident media stars, academics and slew of foreign embassies.

Getting There

Bus Route 1A connects central Copenhagen to Trianglen, the heart of Østerbro. From Vesterbro, Frederiksberg and Nørrebro, route 3A also heads to Trianglen.

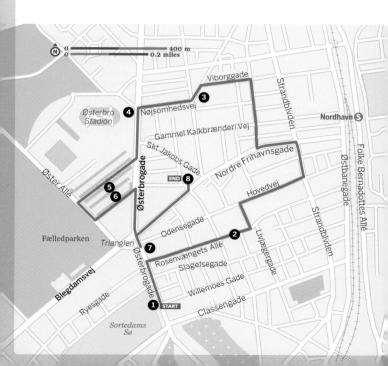

❶ Sortedams Sø

Sortedams Sø (Black Dam Lake) is the most northerly of Copenhagen's trio of central lakes. It's popular with joggers and flâneurs, and a is good spot to sit and reflect.

❷ Rosenvænget

Rosenvænget is the city's oldest suburban development, established in the mid-19th-century. Rosenvaengets Allé 46 was designed by Vilhelm Dahlerup, creator of Ny Carlsberg Glyptotek.

❸ Pixie

Strung with colourful lights, boho cafe **Pixie** (📞39 30 03 05; www.cafepixie.dk; Løgstørgade 2, Østerbro; dishes 55-195kr; 🕙8am-midnight Mon-Thu, to 4am Fri & Sat, 10am-11pm Sun; 🛜; 🚌1A) looks straight off the streets of Buenos Aires. Inside it's a hyggelig affair, with mismatching furniture and candlelight.

❹ Øbro-Hallen

Inspired by the baths of ancient Rome, beautiful **Øbro-Hallen** (📞82 20 51 50; https://svoemkbh. kk.dk/en/node/29; Gunnar Nu Hansens Plads 3, Østerbro; adult/child 40/20kr; 🕙7am-8pm Mon, Tue & Fri, from 8am Wed, from 6.30am Thu, 9am-3pm Sat & Sun; 🚻; 🚌1A) is Denmark's oldest indoor public pool complex (1929–30).

❺ Brumleby

Celebrated Danish writers Martin Andersen Nexø (Pelle the Conqueror) and Peter Høeg (Miss Smilla's Feeling for Snow) have both called Brumleby home. The residential enclave is a heritage-listed combo of yellow-and-white row-housing and cosy gardens.

❻ Olufsvej

Technicolor Olufsvej is lined with 19th-century workers' abodes in a multitude of shades. These days, the properties are home to a number of well-known journalists.

❼ Normann Copenhagen

Sprawling **Normann Copenhagen** (📞35 27 05 40; www.normann-copenhagen.com; Østerbrogade 70, Østerbro; 🕙10am-6pm Mon-Fri, to 4pm Sat; 🚌1A, 14) bursts with must-have design objects, from statement bowls and glassware to furniture, lighting and cushions.

❽ Fischer

Another reformed local is **Fischer** (📞35 42 39 64; www.hosfischer.dk; Victor Borges Plads 12, Østerbro; lunch mains 129-189kr, dinner mains 239kr; 🕙8am-midnight Mon-Fri, from 10am Sat & Sun; 🛜; 🚌3A), a former workingman's bar turned neighbourly trattoria. Owner and head chef David Fischer worked the kitchen at Rome's Michelin-starred La Pergola.

Explore

Vesterbro

Once best known for butchers and sex workers, Vesterbro is now the epicentre of Copenhagen cool. The neighbourhood's hottest corner remains Kødbyen (Meat City), a still-functioning Meatpacking District laced with buzzing eateries, bars, galleries and music venues. Istedgade mixes porn shops with vintage boutiques and ethnic groceries, while further north lies continental Værnedamsvej.

The Short List

○ ***V1 Gallery (p132)*** *Catch an exhibition of edgy contemporary art in the pumping Meatpacking District.*

○ ***Kødbyens Fiskebar (p133)*** *Find sustenance in wild-caught fish, foraged herbs and low-intervention wines in a slick factory conversion.*

○ ***Lidkoeb (p135)*** *Sip reconfigured cocktails and cognoscenti whiskeys in a sneaky, multi-level drinking den.*

○ ***Vega Live (p137)*** *Rock on to on-point indie music acts in a mid-century building by architect Vilhelm Lauritzen.*

○ ***Mikkeller Bar (p136)*** *Slurp top-notch saisons, sours and stouts at Copenhagen's craft beer 'It kid'.*

Getting There & Around

🚌 Routes 6A and 26 run along Vesterbrogade to Frederiksberg Have. Route 9A runs along Gammel Kongevej, connecting Vesterbro to Slotsholmen and Christianshavn.

🚌 Kødbyen lies 500m southwest of Central Station.

Vesterbro Map on p135

Kødbyens Fiskebar (p133) OLLIO815/GETTY IMAGES ©

Walking Tour 🥾

Continental Værnedamsvej

Copenhagers have a soft spot for Værnedamsvej, a sassy little strip they commonly compare to the side streets of Paris. Gallic or not, it is one of Vesterbro's most appealing pockets, dotted with specialist cheese and wine shops, cafes and bistros, petite boutiques and an unmistakably easy, local vibe. Some shops close on the weekends, so head in during the week for the full experience.

Walk Facts

Start Granola
End Prag

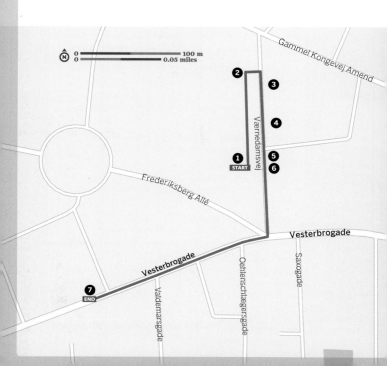

❶ Granola

Granola (📞40 82 41 20; www.
granola.dk; Værndemsvej 5, Frederiksberg; lunch 80-165kr, dinner
mains 145-220kr; ⏱7am-midnight
Mon-Fri, 9am-midnight Sat, 9am-4pm
Sun; 🚌9A, 26, 31, 71) is a staple
of Copenhagen's breakfast and
weekend brunch scene, with a cute
general store-inspired fitout.

❷ Juuls Vin og Spiritus

Vintage wine shop **Juuls Vin og
Spiritus** (📞33 31 13 29; www.juuls.
dk; Værnedamsvej 15, Frederiksberg;
⏱9am-5.30pm Mon-Thu, to 7pm
Fri, to 5pm Sat; 🚌6A, 9A, 31) sells
some thirst-inducing drops, not
to mention an impressive range of
whiskies.

❸ Falernum

Worn floorboards and chairs,
bottled-lined shelves and sooth-
ing tunes give wine bar **Falernum**
(📞33 22 30 89; www.falernum.dk;
Værnedamsvej 16, Vesterbro; ⏱noon-
midnight Sun-Thu, to 2am Fri & Sat; 📶;
🚌6A, 9A, 31) a deliciously moody air.

❹ Samsøe & Samsøe

Originating from the Latin Quarter
and now based in Nørrebro,
Samsøe & Samsøe (📞35 28 51 02;
www.samsoe.com; Værnedamsvej 12,
Vesterbro; ⏱10am-6pm Mon-Thu, to
7pm Fri, to 5pm Sat, 11am-4pm; 🚌6A,
9A, 31) is well known for its contemporary clothing for guys and girls.
This is a label not afraid of unique
patterns, colour and detailing,
and the range includes supremely
comfortable sweat tops, tees and
denim, as well as sharper shirts,
jackets, frocks and outerwear.

❺ Dora

Christian Lacroix notebooks,
quilted laptop covers, hand-
painted lava-stone cheese: design
shop **Dora** (📞32 21 33 57; www.
shopdora.dk; Værnedamsvej 6, Vesterbro; ⏱10am-6pm Mon-Fri, to 4pm Sat,
noon-4pm Sun; 🚌6A, 9A, 31) likes to
keep things highly idiosyncratic,
with harder-to-find objects for any
room and any occasion.

❻ Playtype

Font freaks will go gaga at **Play-
type** (📞60 40 69 14; www.playtype.
com; Værnedamsvej 6, Vesterbro;
⏱noon-6pm Mon-Fri, 11am-3pm
Sat; 🚌6A, 9A, 26), an online type
foundry with its own real-life,
hard-copy shop. The theme is
Danish-designed fonts, showcased
as letters, numbers and symbols on everything from posters,
notebooks and postcards, to crew
necks, raincoats, laptop covers
and mugs.

❼ Prag

Just around the corner from
Værnedamsvej is **Prag** (📞33 79 00
50; www.pragcopenhagen.com; Vesterbrogade 98A, Vesterbro; ⏱10am-6pm
Mon-Fri, to 5pm Sat, noon-5pm Sun;
🚌3A, 6A). It's one of Copenhagen's
funkiest consignment stores, peddling an eclectic booty of clothes
and accessories for both women
and men.

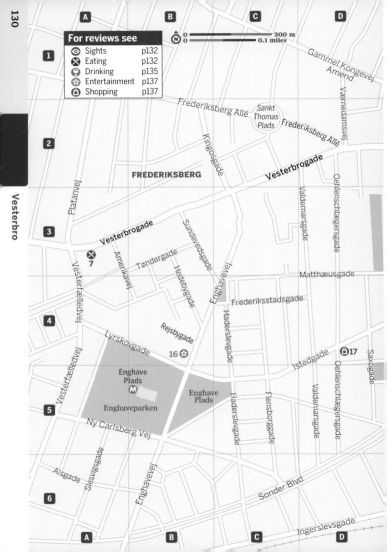

For reviews see

👁	Sights	p132
✖	Eating	p132
🍷	Drinking	p135
⭐	Entertainment	p137
🔒	Shopping	p137

0   200 m
0   0.1 miles

Gammel Kongevej

Amend

Frederiksberg Allé

Sankt Thomas Plads

Frederiksberg Allé

Værnedamsvej

Kingosgade

FREDERIKSBERG

Vesterbrogade

Oehlenschlægersgade

Valdemarsgade

Platanvej

Vesterbrogade

Sundevedsgade

Amerikavej

Vesterfælledvej

✖
7

Tøndergade

Hedebygade

Enghavevej

Matthæusgade

Frederiksstadsgade

Rejsbygade

Lyrskovgade

16 ⭐

Haderslevgade

Istedgade

🔒17

Oehlenschlægersgade

Saxogade

Valdemarsgade

Enghave Plads
Ⓜ

Enghave Plads

Enghaveparken

Ny Carlsberg Vej

Haderslevgade

Flensborggade

Valdemarsgade

Oehlenschlægersgade

Alsgade

Slesvigsgade

Enghavevej

Sønder Blvd

Ingerslevsgade

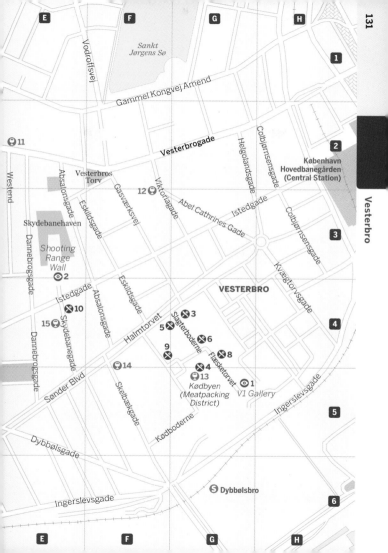

Sights

V1 Gallery
GALLERY

1 ⊙ MAP P130, G5

Part of the Kødbyen (Vesterbro's 'Meatpacking District'), V1 is one of Copenhagen's most progressive art galleries. Cast your eye on fresh work from both emerging and established local and foreign artists. Some of the world's hottest names in street and graffiti art have exhibited here, from Britain's Banksy to the USA's Todd James and Lydia Fong (aka Barry McGee). (☏ 33 31 03 21; www.v1gallery.com; Flæsketorvet 69-71, Vesterbro; admission free; ⊙ noon-6pm Wed-Fri, to 4pm

Street Art Murals

Both Vesterbro and Frederiksberg are home to some huge, spectacular street art murals. Many of these cover the side walls of semi-detached apartment buildings. In Vesterbro, honourable mentions go to Irish artist Conor Harrington's period piece at Tullingsgade 21, Brooklynite Maya Hayuk's geometric statement at Saxogade 7, Belgian artist Roa's furry critters at Gasværksvej 34 and Chinese artist DALeast's giant bird at Oehlenschlægersgade 76. In Frederiksberg, don't miss homegrown Martin Bigum's storybook work at Falkoner Allé 30.

Sat during exhibitions; 🚌 1A, 10, 14, Ⓢ Dybbølsbro)

Shooting Range Wall
HISTORIC SITE

2 ⊙ MAP P130, E3

In a cul-de-sac off Istedgade is this imposing red-brick wall, its gate leading to the delightful Skydebanehaven (Shooting Range Gardens). While it might look medieval, the wall dates back to 1887. At the time, this was the site of the Royal Copenhagen Shooting Society and the wall was built to protect locals from stray bullets. The club's target was parrot shaped, leading to the popular Danish saying 'You've shot the parrot there', used to refer to someone's good fortune.

Today, the playground pays tribute to this past with a parrot-shaped slide. (Istedgade 68-80, Vesterbro; 👬; 🚌 10, 14, Ⓢ København H)

Eating

Paté Paté
INTERNATIONAL $$

3 🍴 MAP P130, G4

This pâté factory turned restaurant/wine bar gives a modern twist to Euro classics. The competent, regularly changing menu is designed for sharing, with smaller dishes like organic Danish burrata with salted courgette, spring onions, chilli, basil and walnuts, or veal tartare with harissa, mustard-pickled shallots and dukkah. Hip and bustling, yet refreshingly convivial, bonus extras

MARY DOGGETT/SHUTTERSTOCK ©

WarPigs (p134)

include clued-up staff, a diverse wine list, and solo-diner-friendly bar seating. (📞39 69 55 57; www.patepate.dk; Slagterboderne 1, Vesterbro; small dishes 95-150kr, 7/9-plate tasting menu 325/385kr; ⏰9am-10pm Mon-Thu, 9am-11pm Fri, 11am-11pm Sat; 🛜; 🚌10, 14)

Kødbyens Fiskebar SEAFOOD $$$

4 ✖ MAP P130, G4

Concrete floors, industrial tiling and a 1000-litre aquarium meet impeccable seafood at this ever-popular, buzzy haunt, slap bang in Vesterbro's trendy Kødbyen (Meatpacking District). Ditch the mains for three or four starters. Standouts include the oysters and lobster with beer meringue, as well as the dainty, delicate razor clams, served on a crisp rice-paper 'shell'. (📞32 15 56 56; www.fiskebaren.dk; Flæsketorvet 100; mains 195-275kr; ⏰5.30pm-midnight Mon-Thu, 11.30am-2am Fri & Sat, 11.30am-midnight Sun; 🛜; 🚌10, 14, Ⓢ Dybbølsbro)

Hija de Sanchez MEXICAN $

5 ✖ MAP P130, F4

Hija de Sanchez serves up fresh, authentic tacos in the Meatpacking District. Expect three rotating varieties daily, from traditional choices like *carnitas* and *al pastor* to 'El Paul' – crispy fish skin with gooseberry salsa. There's always a vegetarian option, as well as homemade Mexican beverages like *tepache* (fermented pineapple juice). Chicago-native chef-owner Rosio Sánchez hails from renowned restaurant Noma, ie

Riding Cykelslangen

Two of the Danes' greatest passions – design and cycling – meet in spectacular fashion with **Cykelslangen**, or Cycle Snake. Designed by local architects Dissing + Weitling, the 235-metre-long cycling path evokes a slender ribbon, its gently curving form contrasting dramatically against the area's block-like architecture. The elevated path winds its way from Bryggebro (Brygge Bridge) west to Fisketorvet Shopping Centre, delivering a cycling experience that's nothing short of whimsical. To reach the path on public transport, catch bus 34 to Fisketorvet Shopping Centre. The best way to reach it, however, is on a bike, as Cykelslangen is only accessible to cyclists.

serious culinary cred. (📞 31 18 52 03; www.hijadesanchez.dk; Slagterboderne 8, Vesterbro; 3 tacos 100kr; ⏱ 11am-8pm Mon-Thu, to 10pm Fri & Sat, to 6pm Sun; 🚌 1A, 10, 14, Ⓢ Dybbølsbro)

Nose2Tail

DANISH $$$

7 🍴 MAP P130, G4

Candlelit industrial tiles, old Danish crockery, crooked old photos: this former basement factory finds its muse in the Danish bars of yesteryear. Here, every part of the animal is used to cook up honest, rustic, made-from-scratch fare. The surf-turf menu is short, seasonal and ethical: the meat is from welfare-minded farms and the produce is mainly organic and from small, local producers. (📞 33 93 50 45; https://nose2tail.dk; Flæsketorvet 13, Vesterbro; mains 250-375kr, 4-course tasting menu 450kr; ⏱ 6pm-1am Mon-Sat; 🛜; 🚌 10, 14)

Pony

NEW NORDIC $$

7 🍴 MAP P130, A3

This is the cheaper, bistro spin-off of Copenhagen's Michelin-starred Kadeau. While the New Nordic grub here is simpler, it's no less nuanced and seasonal; think cured brill with gooseberries and dried brill roe, or roasted wolffish with summer cabbage, black cabbage, nasturtium and crispy grains. The on-point wines are organic and from smaller producers, and the vibe intimate and convivial.

Book ahead, especially on Friday and Saturday. (📞 33 22 10 00; www.ponykbh.dk; Vesterbrogade 135, Vesterbro; 2-/3-/4-course menu 325/425/485kr; ⏱ 5.30-10pm Tue-Sun; 🚌 6A)

WarPigs

BARBECUE $$

8 🍴 MAP P130, G4

Loud, rocking WarPigs satiates carnivores with lusty, American-style barbecue from Europe's biggest meat smokers (capable of smoking up to two tons of meat a day!). Order at the counter, where you can mix and match meats and sides to create a personalised feed. There's also a kicking selection of beers brewed in-house; the place doubles as a brewpub part-owned by local microbrewery **Mikkeller**. (☑43 48 48 48; http://warpigs.dk; Flæsketorvet 25; meat per ¼lb from 45kr; ☺11:30am-midnight Mon-Thu, 11am-2am Fri & Sat, 11am-11pm Sun; ☎; ☐10, 14, S Dybbølsbro)

Tommi's Burger Joint BURGERS $

9 ✖ MAP P130, F4

Hip Iceland export Tommi's Burger Joint sits in the heart of the trendy Meatpacking District. The place is small and packed (consider avoiding peak times), with old-school posters on the walls and music on the stereo. The menu is short, simple and competent: three juicy burgers, a trio of fries and frosty milkshakes to wash it all down. (☑33 31 34 34; www.burgerjoint.dk/kodbyen; Høkerboderne 21-23, Vesterbro; burgers 79-84kr; ☺11am-9pm Mon-Wed, to 10pm Thu-Sun; ☐1A, 10, 14, S Dybbølsbro)

Siciliansk Is ICE CREAM $

10 🍴 MAP P130, E4

Honing their skills in Sicily, gelato meisters Michael and David churn out Copenhagen's (dare we say Denmark's) best gelato. Go for smooth, naturally flavoured options like strawberry, Sicilian blood orange and coconut. For a surprisingly smashing combo, try the *lakrids* (liquorice) with the Sicilian mandarin. *Buonissimo!* (☑30 22 30 89; http://sicilianskis.dk; Skydebane-gade 3, Vesterbro; ice cream from 25kr; ☺noon-9pm mid-May–Aug, 1-6pm Apr–mid-May & Sep; ☐10, 14)

Drinking

Lidkoeb COCKTAIL BAR

11 🅿 MAP P130, E2

Lidkoeb loves a game of hide-and-seek: follow the 'Lidkoeb' signs into the second, light-strung courtyard. Once found, this top-tier cocktail lounge rewards with passionate barstaff and clever, seasonal libations. Slip into a Børge Mogensen chair and toast to Danish ingenuity with Nordic bar bites and seasonal drinks like the Freja's Champagne: a gin-based concoction with

Happening Dyrehaven

Once a spit-and-sawdust working-class bar (the vinyl booths tell the story), **Dyrehaven** (www.dyrehavenkbh.dk; Sønder Blvd 72, Vesterbro; breakfast 30-140kr, lunch 70-95kr, dinner mains 120-195kr; ☺8.30am-2am Mon-Fri, from 9am Sat & Sun; ☎; ☐1A, 10, 14) is now a second home for Vesterbro's cool, young bohemians. Squeeze into your skinny jeans and join them for cheap drinks, simple tasty grub (the 'Kartoffelmad' egg open sandwich is a classic, made with homemade mayo and fried shallots) and DJ-spun tunes on Friday and Saturday nights.

Vega

muddled fresh ginger, lemon and maraschino liqueur.

Extras include a dedicated whisky bar upstairs, open Friday and Saturday nights only. (📞 33 11 20 10; www.lidkoeb.dk; Vesterbrogade 72B, Vesterbro; 🕐 4pm-2am Mon-Sat, from 8pm Sun; 📶; 🚍 6A, 26)

Mikkeller Bar BAR

12 📍 MAP P130, F3

Low-slung lights, green floors and 20 brews on tap: cool, cult-status Mikkeller flies the flag for craft beer, its rotating cast of suds including Mikkeller's own acclaimed creations and guest drops from microbreweries from around the globe. Expect anything from tequila-barrel-aged stouts to

yuzu-infused fruit beers. The bottled offerings are equally inspired, with cheese and snacks to soak up the foamy goodness. (📞 33 31 04 15; http://mikkeller.dk; Viktoriagade 8B-C, Vesterbro; 🕐 2pm-10pm Sun & Mon, to 11pm Tue & Wed, to midnight Thu, to 2am Fri & Sat; 📶; 🚍 6A, 26, Ⓜ København H, Ⓢ København H)

Mesteren & Lærlingen BAR

13 📍 MAP P130, G5

In a previous life, Mesteren & Lærlingen was a slaughterhouse bodega. These days it's one of Copenhagen's in-the-know drinking holes, its tiled walls packing in an affable indie crowd of trucker caps and skinny jeans. Squeeze in and sip good spirits (including a decent mezcal selection) to DJ-spun soul, reggae, hip-hop and dance hall. Wi-fi is available if you ask politely. (www.facebook.com/Mesteren-Lærlin-gen-215687798449433; Flæsketorvet 86, Vesterbro; ⊗8pm-3am Wed & Thu, to 3.30am Fri & Sat; 🛜)

Fermentoren
CRAFT BEER

14 🖭 MAP P130, F4

Serious local beer fans flock to this cosy, candlelit basement bar. Its 24 taps pour an ever-changing cast of interesting craft brews, both traditional and edgy. Look out for local brews from the likes of Evil Twin, Ghost and Gamma, as well as Fermentoren's own pale ale. Staff are extremely knowledgeable, offering expert advice without the attitude. (🗊23 90 86 77; http://fermentoren.com; Halmtorvet 29C, Vesterbro; ⊗3pm-midnight Mon-Wed, 2pm-1am Thu & Fri, 2pm-2am Sat, 2pm-midnight Sun; 🛜; 🚌1A, 10, 14, Ⓢ Dybbølsbro)

Sort Kaffe & Vinyl
CAFE

15 🖭 MAP P130, E4

This skinny little cafe/record store combo is a second home for Vesterbro's coffee cognoscenti. Join them for velvety espresso, hunt down that limited-edition Blaxploitation LP, or score a prized pavement seat and people-watch. (🗊61 70 33 49; Skydebanegade 4, Vesterbro; ⊗8am-9pm Mon-Fri, from 9am Sat & Sun Jul & Aug, 8am-7pm

Mon-Fri, 9am-7pm Sat, 9am-6pm Sun rest of year; 🚌10, 14)

Entertainment

Vega
LIVE MUSIC

16 ✪ MAP P130, B4

The daddy of Copenhagen's live-music venues, Vega hosts everyone from big-name rock, pop, blues and jazz acts to underground indie, hip-hop and electro up-and-comers. Gigs take place on either the main stage (Store Vega), small stage (Lille Vega) or the ground-floor Ideal Bar. Performance times vary; check the website. (🗊33 25 70 11; www.vega.dk; Enghavevej 40, Vesterbro; ⊗varies; 🛜; 🚌3A, 10, 14, Ⓜ Enghave Plads)

Shopping

Kyoto
FASHION & ACCESSORIES

17 🛍 MAP P130, D4

Unisex, multi-brand Kyoto pulls cool hunters with its awesome edits of mostly Nordic labels: think hardy S.N.S. Herning knits, Wrench Monkey shirts, Norse Project tees, Acne Studios denim, as well as Libertine Libertine and Rodebjer frocks. International interlopers include French labels A.P.C. and Kitsuné, while the cast of well-chosen accessories include statement trainers, fragrances and slinky leather wallets. (🗊33 31 66 36; http://kyoto.dk; Istedgade 95, Vesterbro; ⊗10am-6pm Mon-Thu, to 7pm Fri, to 5pm Sat; 🚌10, 14)

Walking Tour 🥾

Frederiksberg Have

Aspiring Copenhageners dream of a Frederiksberg address. Located directly west of Vesterbro, it's a moneyed district, laced with fin-de-siècle architecture, neighbourly bistros and leafy residential streets. It's here that you'll find the landscaped elegance of Frederiksberg Have and the architecturally notable Copenhagen Zoo, as well as one of Copenhagen's finest flea markets.

Getting There

Bus Routes 9A and 31 run past Frederiksberg Rådhus (City Hall). Route 8A runs along the eastern edge of Frederiksberg Have.

Metro Frederiksberg station lies 300m north of Frederiksberg Rådhus.

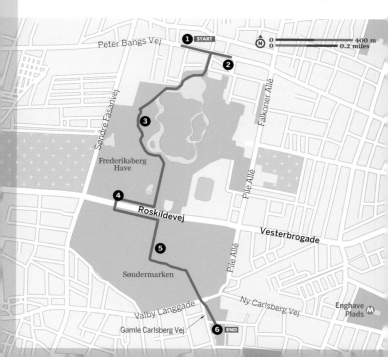

❶ Sokkelund

Classic **Sokkelund** (☑38 10 64 00; http://cafe-sokkelund.dk; Smallegade 36E, Frederiksberg; mains 165-259kr; ⏰8am-11pm Mon-Thu, till 11.30pm Fri, 9am-11.30pm Sat, 9am-10pm Sun; 📶; 🚌8A, 9A, 31, 74, Ⓜ Frederiksberg) is the quintessential neighbourhood brasserie, kitted out with leather banquettes, newspapers on hooks and smart waiters in crisp white shirts.

❷ Frederiksberg Loppetorv

If it's Saturday, scour cult-status flea market **Frederiksberg Loppetorv** (Frederiksberg Flea Market; Smallegade, Frederiksberg Rådhus; ⏰9am-3pm Sat Apr–mid-Oct; 🚌8A, 9A, 31, Ⓜ Frederiksberg). The neighbourhood's affluence is reflected in the quality of the goods, and seasoned treasure hunters head in early for the best finds. There's usually plenty of local and international fashion, with the odd Danish design collectable in the mix.

❸ Frederiksberg Have

Romantic **Frederiksberg Have** (Frederiksberg Runddel, Frederiksberg; ⏰7am-11pm mid-Jun–mid-Aug, to 10pm May–mid-Jun & mid-late Aug, reduced hours rest of year; 🚌6A, 8A, 71, 72, Ⓜ Frederiksberg) woos with its lakes and woodlands. Look out for the Chinese summerhouse pavilion, built in 1803 by court architect Andreas Kirkerup. Overlooking the park is Frederiksborg Slot, a former royal palace, now home to the Royal Danish Military Academy.

❹ Copenhagen Zoo

Perched on Frederiksberg (Frederik's Hill), **Copenhagen Zoo** (☑72 20 02 00; www.zoo.dk; Roskildevej 32, Frederiksberg; adult/child 180/100kr; ⏰10am-6pm Jun & mid-late Aug, to 8pm Jul–mid-Aug, reduced hours rest of year; 🚌6A, 72) rumbles with more than 2500 of nature's lovelies. Its elephant enclosure was designed by English architect Sir Norman Foster, and the newer Arctic Ring enclosure allows visitors to walk right through the polar bear pool.

❺ Cisternerne

Below Søndermarken Park lurks Copenhagen's 19th-century water reservoir. These days it's best known as **Cisternerne** (☑30 73 80 32; www.cisternerne.dk; Søndermarken, Frederiksberg; adult/child 70kr/ free; ⏰11am-6pm Tue, Wed & Fri-Sun, to 8pm Thu mid-Apr-Nov; 🚌6A), one of Copenhagen's most unusual art spaces.

❻ Carlsberg Brewery

Carlsberg Brewery was designed by architect Vilhelm Dahlerup. The brewery's **visitors center** (☑33 27 12 82; www.visitcarlsberg. dk; Gamle Carlsberg Vej 11, Vesterbro; adult/child 100/70kr; ⏰10am-8pm May-Sep, to 5pm rest of year; 🚌1A, 26, Ⓢ Carlsberg) explores the history of Danish beer from 1370 BCE, leading you past antique copper vats and the brewery's famous Jutland dray horses. The self-guided tour ends at the bar, where two free beers await.

Top Experience 📷

Relax in Louisiana's Seaside Sculpture Garden

*Even if you don't have a consuming passion for modern art, Denmark's outstanding **Louisiana Museum of Modern Art** should be high on your 'to do' list. It's a striking modernist gallery, made up of four huge wings, which stretch across a sculpture-filled park, burrowing down into the hillside and nosing out again to wink at the sea (and Sweden).*

📞 49 19 07 19

www.louisiana.dk

Gammel Strandvej 13, Humlebæk

adult/student/child 125/110kr/free

🕐 11am-10pm Tue-Fri, to 6pm Sat & Sun

🚌 388, 🚉 Humlebæk

Getting There

S-Train Louisiana lies in the town of Humlebæk, 30km north of central Copenhagen. From Central Station and Nørreport, S-trains run regularly to Humlebæk station. From here, the museum is a 1.5km signposted walk along Gammel Strandvej.

Don't Miss

Permanent Collection

The museum's permanent collection, mainly postwar paintings and graphic art, covers everything from constructivism, CoBrA movement artists and minimalist art, to abstract expressionism, pop art and staged photography. Pablo Picasso, Francis Bacon and Alberto Giacometti are some of the international luminaries you'll come across inside, while prominent Danish artists include Asger Jorn, Carl-Henning Pedersen, Robert Jacobsen and Richard Mortensen.

Architecture

The Danish architects Vilhelm Wohlert and Jørgen Bo spent several months walking around the grounds before deciding on their design for Louisiana. The result would be one the country's finest examples of modernist architecture, a series of horizontal, light-washed buildings in harmony with their natural surroundings. The museum's three original buildings – completed in 1958 and known as the North Wing – are now accompanied by subsequent extensions. The seats in the Concert Hall are the work of the late designer Poul Kjaerholm.

Sculpture Garden

With views across the deep-blue Øresund to Sweden, Louisiana's arresting grounds are peppered with sculptures from some of the world's most venerated artists. You'll find works from the likes of Max Ernst, Louise Bourgeois, Joan Miró, Henry Moore and Jean Arp, each one positioned to interact with the environment surrounding it.

★ Top Tips

∘ Check the museum website for upcoming events, which include regular evening art lectures and live music.

∘ If you have kids in tow, head to the Children's Wing, where they can create their own masterpieces inspired by the gallery's exhibitions.

✕ Take a Break

With its large sunny terrace and sea views, Louisiana's cultured cafe is a fabulous spot for lunch or a reviving coffee.

Survival Guide

Nyhavn (p77) NIKOLAY ANTONOV/SHUTTERSTCOK ©

Before You Go

Book Your Stay

o The rates of some hostels and most mid-range and top-end hotels are based on supply and demand, with daily fluctuations. In most cases, booking early guarantees the best deal.

o It's a good idea to book in advance – rooms in many of the most popular mid-range hotels fill quickly.

o Copenhagen's hostels often fill early in summer so it's best to make reservations in advance.

o You will need a hostelling card to get the advertised rates at hostels belonging to the Danhostel organisation.

Useful Websites

Lonely Planet (www.lonelyplanet.com/denmark/copenhagen/hotels) Author-reviewed accommodation options.

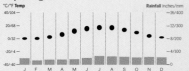

When to Go

o **Spring (March to May)** sees Tivoli Gardens reopen. Weather notoriously sporadic.

o **Summer (June to August)** is peak tourist season, with good weather and festivals. Peak accommodation rates.

o **Autumn (September to November)** sees thinner crowds, autumn foliage and abundant cultural events.

o **Winter (December to February)** brings short days and frigid temperatures. Christmas lights, markets and gløgg (mulled wine) keep spirits up in December.

Eco Hotels (www.eco-hotels.com) Socially conscious booking site that lists sustainable hotels, charges low commissions and plants a tree for every booking made.

Copenhagen Visitors Centre (www.visit-copenhagen.com) Can book last-minute accommodation for visitors for a 100kr booking fee.

Best Budget

Generator Hostel (www.generatorhostel.com) Contemporary dorms, private rooms and a central location.

Copenhagen Downtown Hostel (www.copenhagendowntown.com) Gigs, city walks and free dinners in the historic centre.

Urban House (https://urbanhouse.me) A Vesterbro hostel close to hip eateries and with its own tattoo parlour.

Best Midrange

Hotel Alexandra
(http://hotelalexandra.
dk) A chic yet homey
hotel with cult-status
furniture.

Babette Guldsmeden
(https://guldsmeden
hotels.com) Crisp rooms
and organic breakfasts
near the Royal Palace.

Hotel Danmark (www.
brochner-hotels.com)
Snug, stylish rooms,
free evening vino and a
rooftop terrace.

CPH Living (https://
www.cphliving.com) A
light-filled floating hotel
right on Copenhagen
harbour.

Best Top End

Hotel d'Angleterre
(www.dangleterre.com)
History-steeped luxury
and a celebrity fan base
near Nyhavn.

Hotel Nimb (www.
nimb.dk) Unique luxury
suites with views of a
19th-century pleasure
garden.

**Radisson BLU Royal
Hotel** (www.radis-
sonblue.com) A mid-
century icon created
by design deity Arne
Jacobsen.

Arriving in Copenhagen

Copenhagen Airport

Metro The 24-hour
metro (www.m.dk)
runs every two to 20
minutes between the
airport arrival terminal
(the station is called
Lufthavnen) and tcen-
tral Copenhagen. Alight
at Kongens Nytorv for
Nyhavn or to connect to
the M3 City Circle (City-
ringen) line. Journey
time to Kongens Nytorv
is 14 minutes (36kr).

Train Trains (www.
dsb.dk) connect the
airport arrival terminal
to Copenhagen Central
Station (Københavns
Hovedbanegården,
commonly known as
København H) around
every 10 to 20 minutes.
Journey time is 14
minutes (36kr).

Taxi Journey time
from the airport to the
city centre is about 20
minutes, depending on
traffic. Expect to pay
250kr to 350kr.

Central Station

All regional and inter-
national trains arrive
at and depart from
Central Station located
opposite Tivoli Gardens
in the heart of the city.
Trains run to the airport
every 10 to 20 minutes,
with less frequent
services overnight.

Søndre Frihavn

Søndre Frihavn is
situated 2km north of
central Copenhagen
and serves ferries
to and from Oslo,
Norway. Catch the M4
metro line or an S-train
to Nordhavn station,
from where the port
is a 10- to 15-minute
walk.

Getting Around

Bus

o City buses are fre-
quent, convenient and
run by Movia. If using a
Rejsekort, tap on when
boarding the bus and
tap off when exiting. Buy
single tickets in advance

at 7-Eleven kiosks, from ticket vending machines at train and metro stations, or using the 'DOT Tickets' smartphone app. Single tickets can also be bought onboard from the driver (use small change).

o Primary bus routes have an 'A' after their route number (eg: 1A, 2A) and run around the clock, every three to seven minutes in peak times (7am to 9pm and 3.30pm to 5.30pm) and around every 10 minutes at other times.

o S-buses (buses with an 'S' after their route number) run every five to 10 minutes in peak times and around every 20 minutes at other times. S-buses have fewer stops than A-buses and usually run between 6pm and 1am.

o Night buses (marked with an 'N' after their route number) run between 1am and 5am.

o The free Copenhagen city maps at the tourist office show bus routes (with numbers) and are very useful.

Metro

o Consists of four lines: M1 (green), M2 (yellow),

M3 (red) and M4 (blue). An extension of the M4 is due for completion in 2024.

o Metro trains run around the clock, with a frequency of two to four minutes in peak times, three to six minutes during the day and on weekends, and seven to 20 minutes at night.

o All four lines connect at Kongens Nytorv. The M1, M2 and M3 lines also connect at Frederiksberg, while the M1 and M2 lines also connect at Christianshavn, Nørreport and Forum.

o The M3 line goes to Central Station. The M2 line goes to the airport.

o The rechargeable Rejsekort travel card is valid on the metro.

o See www.m.dk for more information.

Bicycle

o The city-wide rental system **Bycyklen** (City Bikes; www.bycyklen.dk; per hr 30kr) offers high-tech 'Smart Bikes' with GPS, multispeed electric motors and locks. The bikes must by paid for by credit card via the website or the bike's touchscreen.

o Bikes can be carried free on S-trains, but are banned at Nørreport station on weekdays between 7am and 8.30am and between 3.30pm and 5pm. Enter train carriages with the large white bicycle graphic on the windows. Keep your bike behind the line in the designated bicycle area. Stay with the bike at all times.

o Bikes can be carried on the metro (except from 7am to 9am and from 3.30pm to 5.30pm on weekdays). Bike tickets (13kr) are required on metro and city bus services. Purchase bike tickets at metro and S-train stations or using the 'DOT Tickets' app.

Train

o Known locally as S-tog, Copenhagen's suburban train network runs seven lines through Central Station (København H). The S-train runs between Copenhagen Airport and Central Station.

o Services run every four to 20 minutes from approximately 5am to 12.30am. All-night services run hourly on Friday and Saturday (half-hourly on line F).

Tickets & Passes

Copenhagen's bus, metro, S-train and Harbour Bus network has an integrated ticket system based on nine geographical zones. Most of your travel within the city will be within two zones. Travel between the city and airport covers three zones.

The cheapest ticket (*billet*) covers two zones, offers unlimited transfers and is valid for one hour (adult/12 to 15 years 24/12kr). An adult with a valid ticket can take two children under the age of 12 free of charge.

Alternatively, you can purchase a Rejsekort (www.rejsekort.dk), a touch-on, touch-off smart card valid for all zones. Available from the Rejsekort machines at metro stations, Central Station or the airport, the card costs 180kr (80kr for the card and 100kr in credit). Various ticket types (including single tickets) can be bought using the 'DOT Tickets' smartphone app.

The tourist-saver **Copenhagen Card** (www.copenhagencard.com; adult/child 10-15yr 24hr 419/209kr, 48hr 619/309kr, 72hr 759/379kr, 96hr 889/449kr, 120hr 999/499kr) includes unlimited public transport throughout the greater region of Copenhagen (including the airport).

○ The rechargeable Rejsekort travel card is valid on S-train services.

Boat

○ Movia operates the city's yellow commuter ferries, known as Harbour Buses.

○ Route 991 runs south along the harbour, 992 runs north. There are eight harbour stops, including Det Kongelige Bibliotek (Royal Library), Nyhavn and Operaen (Opera House).

○ Route 993 serves as a shuttle service between Nyhavn and Operaen.

○ The rechargeable Rejsekort travel card is valid on Harbour Buses.

Essential Information

Accessible Travel

○ Copenhagen, and Denmark in general, are improving accessibility all the time, although accessibility is still not ubiquitous. The official www.visitcopenhagen. com website lists accessible attractions, stations, hotels and hostels, as well as practical tips and useful links. To access the page, click on 'Planning', then 'Accessible Copenhagen'.

○ A useful resource is God Adgang (Good Access; www.godadgang. dk), which lists service providers who have had their facilities registered and labelled for accessibility.

Business Hours

Opening hours vary throughout the year. We've provided high-season opening

Money-Saving Tips

o Some museums offer free entry, either daily or once weekly.

o Seniors and students qualify for discounts on some transport fares and museum entry fees, but you'll need to show proof of student status or age.

o Self-catering at supermarkets and markets can help keep food costs down.

o Consider getting around on foot – compact Copenhagen was made for walking.

hours; hours generally decrease in the shoulder and low seasons.

Banks 10am–4pm Monday to Friday (to 5.30pm or 6pm Thursday)

Bars 4pm–midnight, to 2am or later Friday and Saturday (clubs on weekends may open until 5am)

Boutiques 10am or 11am–6pm Monday to Friday, to 4pm Saturday, some open Sunday

Cafes 8am–5pm or 6pm

Department Stores 10am–8pm

Restaurants noon–10pm or 11pm

Supermarkets 8am–9pm or 10pm (some open 7am; a few open 24 hours)

COVID-19

COVID-19-vaccinated travellers can generally enter Denmark freely. Check https://en.coronasmitte.dk for the latest government guidelines, restrictions and entry requirements.

Discount Cards

The **Copenhagen Card** (www.copenhagencard.com; adult/child 10-15yr 24hr 419/209kr, 48hr 619/309kr, 72hr 759/379kr, 96hr 889/449kr, 120hr 999/499kr) gives you access to over 80 museums and attractions, as well as free public transport. Each adult card includes up to two children aged under 10. The card can be purchased online,

at the Copenhagen Visitors Centre, as well as at the airport information desk, the tourist information centre inside Central Station, and at various hotels and 7-Eleven stores.

Electricity

Type C
220V/50Hz

Money

Credit Cards

o Credit cards such as **Visa** (☑80 01 02 77; www.visa.dk) and **MasterCard** (☑80 01 60 98; www.mastercard.com) are widely accepted in Denmark (**American Express** (AMEX; ☑70 14 21 92; www.americanexpress.com) and **Diners Club** (☑36 73 72

Dos & Don'ts

○ Cycling Rules Brush up on cycling rules *before* you start pedaling.

○ Crossing the Street Wait for the man to turn green, even if the road is clear.

○ Punctuality Trains and tours run on time. Danes operate similarly in social situations.

○ Queuing Machines dispensing numbered tickets are common at places where queues might form. Grab a ticket and wait your turn.

○ Toasts Raise your glass, say *skål* (cheers!) and make eye contact with everyone.

39; www.dinersclub.com) less so).

○ In many places (hotels, petrol stations, restaurants, shops) a surcharge may be imposed on foreign cards (up to 3.75%). If there is a surcharge, it must be advertised (eg on the menu, at reception).

Public Holidays

New Year's Day (Nytårsdag) 1 January

Maundy Thursday (Skærtorsdag) Thursday before Easter

Good Friday (Langfredag) Friday before Easter

Easter Day (Påskedag) Sunday in March or April

Easter Monday (2. påskedag) Day after Easter

Great Prayer Day (Stor Bededag) Fourth Friday after Easter

Ascension Day (Kristi Himmelfartsdag) Sixth Thursday after Easter

Whitsunday (Pinsedag) Seventh Sunday after Easter

Whitmonday (2. pinsedag) Seventh Monday after Easter

Constitution Day (Grundlovsdag) 5 June

Christmas Eve (Juleaften) 24 December (from noon)

Christmas Day (Juledag) 25 December

Boxing Day (2. juledag) 26 December

Safe Travel

Copenhagen is a very safe city, but you should always employ common sense.

○ Keep your belongings in sight, particularly in busy places.

○ Keep clear of the busy bike lanes that run beside roads; they are easy to wander onto (and straight into the path of cyclists).

Toilets

○ Public toilets are generally easy to find and most are free to use.

○ Handy places to find them include department stores, libraries and major train stations.

○ Museums, cafes and restaurants have toilets for their guests.

Tourist Information

Copenhagen Visitors Centre (☏ 70 22 24 42; www.visitcopenhagen.com; Vesterbrogade 4A; 📶; 🚃 2A, 5C, 6A, 12, 14, 26, Ⓜ København H, Ⓢ København H) Copenhagen's excellent and informative information centre has a cafe and lounge with free wi-fi; it also sells the **Copenhagen Card** (www.copenhagencard.com; adult/child 10-15yr 24hr 419/209kr, 48hr 619/309kr, 72hr 759/379kr, 96hr 889/449kr, 120hr 999/499kr).

Visas

Citizens or Residents of EU & Schengen Countries No visa required.

Citizens or Residents of the UK, USA, Canada, Australia, New Zealand, most Latin American and some Asian Countries No visa required for tourist stays of less than 90 days. From 1 January 2023, nationals of these countries will require pre-authorisation to enter Denmark under the new European Travel Information and Authorisation System (ETIAS); see www.etias.com.

Other Countries Citizens of many African and some Latin American, Asian and former Soviet bloc countries require a visa; see www.nyidanmark.dk.

Responsible Travel

Overtourism

o Travel off-season: outside summer months (mid-Jun–Aug) and Christmas, and mid-week instead of weekends.

o Consider ditching apartment lets for a hotel; not only do hotels support local jobs and help prevent long-term soaring rents for locals, most hotel rooms in Copenhagen hold an official eco-certification.

o Stay more than a couple of days. Explore Zealand's atmospheric coastal towns and villages, historic Roskilde, or spend a night at a sustainable gourmet destination like Dragsholm Slot (www.dragsholm-slot.dk).

o Check Visit Copenhagen (www.visitcopenhagen.com) and Visit Denmark (www.visitdenmark.com) for tips and resources on responsible, sustainable travel in the city.

Support Ethical & Local

Consult the GoGreen Danmark website (www.gogreendanmark.dk) or download the GoGreen Danmark app for a list of sustainable local businesses, from organic, climate-friendly eateries to ethical fashion boutiques.

Tread Lightly

o Do as the Copenhageners do and get around town on a bike. The city's cycling network is the world's best and bike rental is widely available. This includes public bike-sharing scheme Bycyklen (www.bycyklen.dk).

o Reduce waste by refilling your water bottle at one of the city's 60-plus drinking fountains; the local water is fresh and clean.

Language

Most of the sounds in Danish have equivalents in English, and by reading our pronunciation guides as if they were English, you're sure to be understood. There are short and long versions of each vowel, and additional 'combined vowels' or diphthongs. Consonants can be 'swallowed' and even omitted completely, creating (together with vowels) a glottal stop or *stød steudh* which sounds rather like the Cockney pronunciation of the 'tt' in 'bottle'. Note that *ai* is pronounced as in 'aisle', *aw* as in 'saw', *eu* as the 'u' in 'nurse', *ew* as the 'ee' in 'see' with rounded lips, *ow* as in 'how', *dh* as the 'th' in 'that', and *r* is trilled. The stressed syllables are in italics in our pronunciation guides.

To enhance your trip with a phrasebook, visit **lonelyplanet.com**.

Basics

Hello.
Goddag.　　　　　　go·*da*

Goodbye.
Farvel.　　　　　　faar·*vel*

Yes./No.
Ja./Nej.　　　　　　ya/nai

Please.
Vær så venlig.　　　ver saw *ven*·lee

Thank you.
Tak.　　　　　　　　taak

You're welcome.
Selv tak.　　　　　　sel taak

Excuse me.
Undskyld mig.　　　awn·skewl mai

Sorry.
Undskyld.　　　　　awn·skewl

How are you?
Hvordan går det?　　vor·*dan* gawr dey

Good, thanks.
Godt, tak.　　　　　got taak

What's your name?
Hvad hedder du?　　va *hey*·dha doo

My name is ...
Mit navn er ...　　　mit nown ir ...

Do you speak English?
Taler du engelsk?　　*ta*·la dee/doo *eng*·elsk

I don't understand.
Jeg forstår ikke.　　yai for·*stawr i*·ke

Eating & Drinking

What would you recommend?
Hvad du anbefale?　　va doo *an*·bey·fa·le

Do you have vegetarian food?
Har I vegetarmad?　　haar ee vey·ge·*taar*·madh

Cheers!
Skål!　　　　　　　skawl

I'd like (the) ..., please.
Jeg vil gerne have ..., tak.　　yai vil *gir*·ne ha ... taak

　　bill
　　regningen　　　　*rai*·ning·en

Emergencies

Help!
Hjælp! — yelp

Go away!
Gå væk! — gaw vek

Call ...!
Ring efter ...! — ring ef·ta ...

  a doctor
  en læge — in le·ye

  the police
  politiet — poh·lee·tee·et

It's an emergency!
Det er et nødstilfælde!
dey ir it — neudhs·til·fe·le

I'm lost.
Jeg er faret vild. — yai ir faa·ret veel

I'm sick.
Jeg er syg. — yai ir sew

It hurts here.
Det gør ondt her. — dey geur awnt heyr

I'm allergic to...
Jeg er allergisk — yai ir a·ler·geesk
over for... — o·va for...

Where's the toilet?
Hvor er toilettet? — vor ir toy·le·tet

Shopping & Services

I'm looking for ...
Jeg leder efter ... — yai li·dha ef·ta ...

How much is it?
Hvor meget — vor maa·yet
koster det? — kos·ta dey

Can I have a look?
Må jeg se? — maw yai sey

Time & Numbers

What time is it?
Hvad er klokken? — va ir klo·ken

1	*en*	in
2	*to*	toh
3	*tre*	trey
4	*fire*	feer
5	*fem*	fem
6	*seks*	seks
7	*syv*	sew
8	*otte*	aw·te
9	*ni*	nee
10	*ti*	tee
100	*hundrede*	hoon·re·dhe
1000	*tusind*	too·sen

Transport & Directions

Where's the ...?
Hvor er ...? — vor ir ...

What's the address?
Hvad er adressen? — va ir a·draa·sen

How do I get there?
Hvordan kommer — vor·dan ko·ma
jeg derhen? — yai deyr·hen

Please take me to (this address).
Vær venlig at — ver ven·lee at
køre mig — keu·re mai
til (denne adresse). — til (de·ne a·draa·se)

Please stop here.
Venligst stop her. — ven·leest stop heyr

boat	*båden*	baw·dhen
bicycle	*cykel*	see·kel
bus	*bussen*	boo·sen
plane	*flyet*	flew·et
train	*toget*	taw·et

Behind the Scenes

Send Us Your Feedback

We love to hear from travellers – your comments help make our books better. We read every word, and we guarantee that your feedback goes straight to the authors. Visit **lonelyplanet.com/contact** to submit your updates and suggestions.

Note: We may edit, reproduce and incorporate your comments in Lonely Planet products such as guidebooks, websites and digital products, so let us know if you don't want your comments reproduced or your name acknowledged. For a copy of our privacy policy visit lonelyplanet.com/privacy.

Cristian's Thanks

For their priceless insight, generosity and friendship, *tusind tak* to Martin Kalhøj, Mette Cecilie Smedegaard, Christian Struckmann Irgens, Mads Lind, Mia Hjorth Lunde and Jens Lunde, Mary-ann Gardner and Lambros Hajisava, Sophie Lind and Kasper Monrad, Anne Marie Nielsen, Sanna Klein Hedegaard Hansen and Carolyn Bain. In-house, many thanks to Gemma Graham.

Acknowledgements

Cover photograph: Nyhavn canal, Maurizio Rellini/AWL Images ©; back photograph: Smørrebrød selection, Sarah Coghill/Lonely Planet ©

Photographs p34-5: Roland Magnusson/shutterstock ©; Perekotypole/shutterstock ©

This Book

This 5th edition of Lonely Planet's *Pocket Copenhagen* was written by Cristian Bonetto, as was the previous edition. This guidebook was produced by the following:

Senior Product Editor Angela Tinson

Product Editor Grace Dobell

Cartographers Valentina Kremenchutskaya, Julie Sheridan

Book Designer Clara Monitto

Cover Researcher Gwen Cotter

Assisting Editors Imogen Bannister, Michelle Bennett, Katie Connolly, Barbara Delissen, Victoria Harrison, Jodie Martire, Kristin Odijk, Genna Patterson, Mani Ramaswamy, Maja Vatrić

Thanks to Claire Naylor, Kirsten Rawlings, Jessica Ryan

Index

See also separate subindexes for:

⊗ **Eating p155**

🍷 **Drinking p155**

✪ **Entertainment p156**

🔒 **Shopping p156**

Index

Sights 000
Map Pages 000

Notes

Our Writers

Cristian Bonetto

Cristian has contributed to over 30 Lonely Planet guides to date, including *New York City, Italy, Venice & the Veneto, Naples & the Amalfi Coast, Denmark, Copenhagen, Sweden* and *Singapore*. Lonely Planet work aside, his musings on travel, food, culture and design appear in numerous publications around the world, including *The Telegraph* (UK) and *Corriere del Mezzogiorno* (Italy). When not on the road, you'll find the reformed playwright and TV scriptwriter slurping espresso in his beloved hometown, Melbourne. Instagram: rexcat75.

Published by Lonely Planet Global Limited
CRN 554153
5th edition – April 2022
ISBN 978 1 78701 620 0
© Lonely Planet 2022 Photographs © as indicated 2022
10 9 8 7 6 5 4 3 2 1
Printed in Malaysia